AFRICAN GREYS

First Edition

by

Fran Gonzalez

Published by
Neon Pet Publications
P.O. Box 733
Cypress, California 90630-0733

Library of Congress Catalog Card Number: 95-92568

ISBN 0-9637844-1-2

Table of Contents

4

Chapter 13, Continued

Chapter 17, Continued

Introduction

African Grey Parrots are one of the most sought-after talking parrots in the world. In the past, young and older imported birds were sold from quarantine stations to pet stores and jobbers (middlemen) who, in turn, sold these birds to the public. Most of these birds were extremely wild and many were untamable. Today, these same birds are still not tame, but excellent talkers. Breeders were anxious to buy mature wild-caught birds to set up in captive breeding programs.

In the mid to late eighties, hand-fed African Greys started becoming more in demand. Bird owners were thrilled to be able to cuddle, hand-feed and bond with their bird. As these birds matured, they became more independent, and excellent talkers. As more and more people acquired these birds, their behavior became more interesting, and sometimes puzzling. Some birds that were upset by a change in their home environment started nervous behaviors, while other birds that seemed quite content also displayed similar behaviors.

No matter how ornery or how imperfect these birds may become, their owners are usually not willing to part with them, for many reasons, which will be discussed in this book. This book will explore all African Grey Parrots: the Congo, the Ghana (also known as the West African Grey), and the Timneh. It will focus on hand-raised birds, but wild-caught birds and their traits will also be discussed. This book will help a new grey owner, and provide guidance for soon-to-be grey owners. It is our hope that all African Grey lovers will find this the most complete source of information about one of the most intelligent parrot species.

Neon Pet Publications

Note: To make this book more informative and complete, Ms. Gonzalez has utilized information from an informal survey completed by actual African Grey owners. All of the additional observations and theories are those that she has learned about African Greys in the last twelve years.

The male Congo African Grey is many times a darker shade of gray, while the female may be a lighter gray.

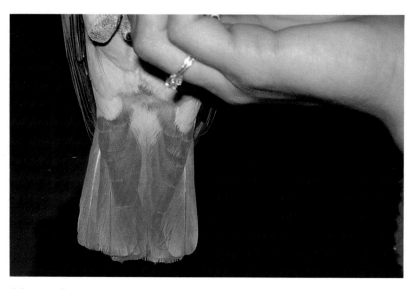

Mature female Congo African Greys have grey tips on the covert feathers under the tail.

Chapter 1

Vital Statistics

It is important to know a little bit of vital information about the African Grey Parrots: Where they come from, what type of climate they live in, and how the different subspecies compare to each other.

The Latin name for the entire African Grey parrot family is *Psittacus erithacus*. Their distribution ranges from Central Africa from the Gulf of Guinea Islands and the west coast towards western Kenya and northwestern Tanzania. In 1991, my husband, Omar, traveled to Africa with our friend Steve Garvin to observe the greys in their native habitat. They traveled first to the Ivory Coast, where they saw West African and Timneh Greys for sale in the marketplace, then to Senegal, and finally to Cameroon where they observed Congo African Greys in the wild, and Timneh African Greys in captivity.

According to Joseph M. Forshaw, in his book, *Parrots of the World*, there are only three subspecies of the African Grey:

Psittacus erithacus erithacus: which is the Congo African Grey.

Psittacus erithacus princeps: which is a "supposed" separate species of African Grey that comes from the islands of Principe'. When Omar and Steve went to Africa they were unable to locate anyone with information about these birds.

Psittacus erithacus timneh: this is of course, the Timneh African Grey.

The African Grey parrots that are available today can be separated into three groups, however, they are usually referred to as the Congo African Grey, West African Grey (or Ghana), and the Timneh African Grey. I don't know if Forshaw had information regarding the West African Greys, but they are slightly different from the Congos.

The Congo African Grey

The largest of all of the African Greys, the Congo is tall and buffed, measuring around 12 inches (30.5 cm.) from head to tail. There are usually differences between males and females; males are usually slightly larger and have a flat, square head.

Males are also darker shades of gray, and the red covert feathers under the tail are solid red in a mature bird. (A mature bird is one that is over two years old.) The covert feathers above the tail are also usually solid red. Female Congos typically are lighter shades of gray, some almost powder-white, and their heads are more round in shape. Mature female Congos have grey tips on the covert feathers under the tail. The female's neck is long and slender, while the male's neck is short and stout. Some female Congos have almond shaped eyes, while the male's eye shape is more round.

Congo African Greys are the most well-known for their elegant looks, large size, and talking ability.

The average weight for an adult Congo is around 450-500 grams.

The Ghana, or West African Grey, is considerably smaller than the Congo, and males and females are a darker shade of gray.

Ghana, or West African Greys

These birds are not too different from the Congo, the main difference is in their size. If you place a Ghana and a Congo on the same perch, the Ghana is usually a full two inches shorter. The average length of the Ghana is 10 inches (25.4 cm.) from head to tail. Many pet owners and breeders don't even know they have a Ghana until they see another grey that is much larger than theirs.

Ghanas also have a slightly different shape to their head and their body. Ghana African Greys are usually darker shades of gray, and determining males and females is not as easy as it is with the Congos. Ghanas are just as intelligent and are excellent talkers; the only real difference between these birds and the Congos is their size.

The average weight for an adult Ghana is 350-400 grams.

Timnehs are just as good at talking as the larger greys!

Timneh African Greys

There is very little information written about Timneh African Greys; they always seem to be overshadowed by their larger relatives. Many people even believe that Timnehs don't make good talkers, which couldn't be farther from the truth! The average Timneh African Grey measures about 9 inches (22.9 cm.) from head to tail, and the tail is a dark burgundy color; sometimes it looks like black or dark gray overtones on top of burgundy. A wild-caught Timneh can be one of the most difficult birds to train, and slow to talk, however a hand-raised Timneh is super sweet and lovable and destined to be an excellent talker.

I have noticed that Timnehs are not as insecure as the larger Greys, and they handle stress a little easier than the bigger birds. Timnehs are more difficult to breed than the Congos and Ghanas, and are not as readily available. It is possible that in the future these birds may be worth more than their larger counterparts.

The average weight for an adult Timneh is 290 grams.

11

Eye Color

All baby African Greys are born with dark coal grey eyes. As they grow, the color of the iris lightens, and when the bird is fully mature, around two to four years, it is a yellowish white. Generally, the eye color is as follows:

Eyes opening to 6 months	- Dark grey or black
6 months - 1 year	- Light grey
1 year - 2 years	- Beige
2 years +	- Yellowish-Beige to Yellow

Life Expectancy

It is believed that the average life expectancy of the African Grey Parrot is around 40-60 years; there are not many documented records to refer to, and most of the pet birds in captivity today have been around an average of 5-10 years. There is a large population of pet African Greys that is under five years of age at this time. It will be interesting to gather information on this generation of greys to see if their life expectancy figures change.

All of the information in this book will apply to the Congo, the West African, and Timneh Grey; any specific individual traits will be noted.

Chapter 2

Choosing the Right Bird

If you are contemplating purchasing an African Grey Parrot, you may already have your heart set on a Congo, or you may be attracted to the Timneh because it is slightly smaller in size. If you are not sure at all, the best thing to do is to visit your local bird store and try to arrange to see both sizes of birds. If you are not familiar with any of the bird vendors in your area, consult with your avian veterinarian to see if they can recommend a breeder or source for healthy birds.

The primary concerns when purchasing a baby African Grey should be:
- Personality of the Bird
- Health Guarantee
- Follow-up Guidance
- Grooming/Maintenance Services
- Price

Personality of the Bird

If you are looking at a very young African Grey, it may not have much of a personality yet. Some babies may even growl at you when you try to touch them! Don't worry, this is a built-in defense mechanism for African Greys in the wild-if they growl loud enough, a possible predator may back off and leave them alone. Growling is not a learned behavior, but a natural instinct. We have had incubator-raised babies also growl when they are frightened. All of the imported African Greys were known for their ominous growling anytime a human would approach their cage.

Baby African Greys start developing a personality around seven weeks of age; at this time they like to whine for attention and will let you pet them just about anywhere. The cuddly stage is usually short-lived, however, and by the time the bird is weaned (stops eating formula from a syringe or spoon), which is around 12-14 weeks, it may not want to be cuddled or petted as much.

The best time to buy a baby African Grey is before it weans, as long as you have the desire to hand-feed the bird once or twice a day. Baby Greys are the easiest birds to learn how to syringe-feed, because they lap the food up in small bites.

Health Guarantee

What type of health guarantee should you ask for? One that you understand, and one that is in writing. Most breeders offer anywhere from 24 - 72 hours for the buyer to take the bird to an avian veterinarian for a cursory exam. Birds that are shipped via airlines are usually only guaranteed for live arrival only, because there are so many additional factors involved in the delivery of the bird. Keep in mind that if you intend to have your avian veterinarian perform any lab work, those results may not come in for at least 3 - 5 days, and some tests may take longer. Will your breeder or pet store honor the veterinarian's report and extend your guarantee? (Generally, some stores will, while others stick to the time written on the guarantee.) It may be less money in the long run if you do business with a reputable establishment in the event you have problems with the bird.

Choosing a Healthy Bird

The only way to know for certain that a bird is healthy is to take the bird to an avian veterinarian and have him or her give the bird a thorough exam, which includes cultures and blood work. Lab work will be discussed in Chapter 3; for now we will discuss things to look for when buying an African Grey.

Feather Quality-The plumage, or feathers, should be clean and smooth. Feathers should not be broken, paler than normal, or contain stress lines. Some baby African Greys have red feathers mixed in with the grey feathers, and some have a reddish tint to their feathers; this is not anything rare, and these feathers are usually replaced by normal gray feathers with the first and second molt.

If you are purchasing a young bird, the feathers should be soft and smooth. If you are purchasing an older bird, and the bird appears to be missing some feathers, it may have chewed or plucked the feathers. In a sexually mature bird, imperfect feathering will have no impact whatsoever on the bird's ability to breed. Some birds chew their feathers out of boredom, or to relieve stress (more on this later!).

You must be careful not to confuse feather chewing or plucking with feather loss, which is much more serious. Feather loss can be caused by a thyroid imbalance or Psittacine Beak and Feather Syndrome (PBFD).

Important: An African Grey has to be exposed to PBFD in order to get it; if the bird has not been around other birds, and the parents do not have PBFD, then the babies will not have PBFD.

Follow-up Guidance

It is especially important to know if you may call the breeder or pet store for any questions, concerns, or needs that may arise. Some breeders will refer you to a knowledgable source for information, while others do not mind if you call them with questions. Most reputable dealers want to hear from you and appreciate you calling them even if you think there might be a problem, so don't hesitate to find answers to your questions.

Grooming

Many pet stores offer complimentary grooming if you purchase your bird from their store; others offer grooming at a nominal charge. If you are not going to groom your bird yourself, then you must take into consideration the expense of grooming the bird into your budget.

Price

I intentionally placed this item last, because it should not be the primary influence when choosing your African Grey. The place you decide to purchase your bird should be clean, the birds should be well cared for, and the price should be close to the current market value for the bird.

Chapter 3

Going to the Vet

Okay, so you found a bird you like, and you plan to take it to an avian veterinarian as soon as possible to be sure that it is healthy. What tests should you do? What about shots? There are so many things to learn about birds in general, going to the vet can be confusing.

Important: If you are taking a baby African Grey to the veterinarian for weighing or a full exam, be sure to take it with an empty crop! The reason for this is: (1) the bird could aspirate (choke) on formula in the crop while it is being handled, and (2) if the veterinarian wants to do a culture and sensitivity on the crop, it will be more accurate if the crop is empty.

Physical Exam

During a physical exam, the veterinarian looks at the bird's overall appearance, feather quality, weight and mouth. During this exam, the veterinarian should:

- Weigh your bird.
- Look in your bird's mouth.
- Check to be sure the bird's notrils are clear.
- Check to be sure the bird's eyes are bright.
- Look at your bird's abdomen and vent.
- Listen to your bird's heart, lungs and air sacs.
- Recommend health-screening tests, if needed.

Birds have gram-positive and gram-negative bacteria present in their systems. Gram-positive bacteria is usually acceptable in a bird, and does not usually cause a bird to become ill. A light to moderate amount of gram-negative bacteria is usually acceptable, unless it is a potentially dangerous bacteria such as *Salmonella, Pseudomonas or Klebsiella*, but a heavy or an abundant amount is not acceptable. Always ask your veterinarian for a copy of the culture and sensitivity report; it will list what type of bacteria your bird has and if it is gram-positive or gram-negative, and what drugs are sensitive to the bacteria.

When a bird shows signs of illness such as a runny nose, fluffed feathers, runny stools, weight loss or lethargy, it is clinically ill.

Remember: Baby greys that are very young will lay on their sides to sleep and basically only eat and sleep while they are still growing.

Some perfectly healthy looking birds will culture out with a moderate to heavy bacterial infection; this is known as a sub-clinical infection. In the wild, birds hide their illnesses to avoid being abandoned by their flock and attracting predators. In captivity, birds are known for this same behavior. Stress can reduce a bird's natural ability to fight a bacteria or virus. The following situations may stress a bird:

- Changing the baby's hand-feeder
- Changing the baby's hand-feeding formula
- Bathing a bird improperly
- Changing its diet
- Moving the bird from one home to another
- A sudden change in temperature
- Changing the bird's routine
- Grooming
- A health exam

Gram's Stain

A Gram's stain is a simple procedure in which the veterinarian swabs a surface, usually the throat (called the choanal slit), or the bird's vent, a stool sample, nasal discharge, an unhatched egg or a baby.

The veterinarian then smears one or more glass slides with the swab and follows a procedure in which the slide is flooded with several solutions and rinsed accordingly. The end result is a slide the veterinarian can look at under the microscope to view the possible ratio of gram-positive vs. gram-negative bacteria. If the Gram's stain reflects normal levels of bacterial flora in a healthy-looking bird, no other testing should be necessary. If the Gram's stain appears to indicate a bacterial infection, and the bird is not clinically ill, it is best to do a culture and sensitivity instead of guessing which antibiotics would be most effective. Of course, if the bird displays signs of illness, antibiotics should be prescribed, and could save its life.

During an initial health check we do not use the Gram's stain on any of our birds; we prefer to have our veterinarian do a complete culture and sensitivity.

Culture and Sensitivity

To more accurately check your bird's bacterial levels, you can have the veterinarian do a culture and sensitivity. The veterinarian swabs the roof of the bird's mouth (or other site) and then wipes the swab on a prepared bacteria culture plate. The plate is labeled and sealed and sent to a laboratory. At the lab, they put the plate in an incubator and see what type of bacteria grows. After about 48-72 hours, the lab identifies the types of bacteria present and determines if the growth is light, moderate or heavy.

They then test the bacteria with antibiotics to see which antibiotics are most effective. Many types of bacteria resist antibiotics. This is why it is important not to indiscriminately give antibiotics to your birds; it's too easy to give a bird an antibiotic that may not be effective for that bird's illness. A correct antibiotic at the wrong dose can cause the bacteria to develop a resistance to it.

A culture and sensitivity usually takes about 3-4 days. Many veterinarians now do their own cultures, which can speed up the process. Request a copy of the lab report so you can familiarize yourself with the test, its results and the drugs that will be effective against it.

It is not uncommon for birds to have mild bacterial infections, especially baby birds. More serious infections may require oral or injectable treatments. If a bird cultures out with low levels of gram-negative bacteria but is otherwise healthy, we do not treat them with antibiotics. Usually, the bird's natural immune system will begin to work and if the bird is cultured one or two months later, the bacteria may be gone. If we cultured our own mouths, they would be loaded with bacteria. Similarly, bird's mouths contain natural, bacterial flora.

Fecal Exam

It is also important to take a fresh stool sample to your veterinarian and have him or her examine it for internal parasites (worms). Imported African Greys were known for carrying tapeworms, however, most domestic birds are free of this problem. The test is inexpensive, so it wouldn't hurt to check just in case. Stool samples can be looked at under a microscope or checked by a flotation test for parasite eggs or worms. There are no false positives with this test, but birds can act as carriers, causing occasional false negatives. (Once again, domestic birds are rarely carriers.)

Avian Blood Tests

Depending upon how much information you want and how much money you want to spend, you can learn a lot from your bird's blood profile.

Most veterinarians perform a simple CBC, or complete blood count, when they examine healthy-looking birds. This test checks the white and red cell count. An elevated white cell count may indicate an infection, and you may wish to have the veterinarian do further testing.

Important Note: A slightly elevated white count can be caused by the stress of the visit to the veterinarian, so if all the other tests check out okay, the bird is probably fine. Be sure the veterinarian or technician doesn't "milk" the bird's toe when he or she takes the blood sample; it can affect the results. Some veterinarians prefer to take blood from the jugular or wing veins; I prefer the toenail, because it is not as risky.

Full Avian Blood Panel

A full avian blood panel will tell you everything from the red and white blood-cell count to the bird's calcium level, liver enzymes, uric acid and more. This is one of the most complete tests you can do on a bird. It is also more expensive. African Greys are prone to have calcium deficiencies, so this may be a test you wish to consider for a newly purchased bird of that species.

Psittacosis Testing

Psittacosis, or *Clamydia psittaci*, is very common among imported birds and is easily treated if detected early. Psittacosis can be transmitted from one bird to another bird and from birds to humans, but it cannot be transmitted from human to human or human to bird. (In humans, the symptoms resemble a very bad respiratory flu that won't go away.)

Birds can carry Psittacosis for years, without appearing ill. Sometimes sick birds will exhibit bright, lime-green stools; others will show no signs at all.

Many methods are used to test for Psittacosis; the most common at this time are the Clamydia Antigen Test, and the Psittacosis Antibody Test.

Psittacosis can be a very tricky organism to test for, and false negatives as well as false positives are common. The antibody test, which is a blood titer, is the method we prefer. A blood sample is sent out and the number of antibodies present indicates if the bird could possibly have been exposed to, or be a carrier of Psittacosis. A high number of antibodies could mean that your bird was recently exposed, and your veterinarian may recommend you have the bird re-tested in 30 days, providing the bird is acting fine and is otherwise healthy.

If the bird in question is clinically ill, a Clamydia Antigen, or swab test, is quicker and easier. Many avian veterinarians do this test in their own office and even if they don't, the results are available within hours. The only drawback to this test is that it can give a false negative reading if the bird is not shedding the organism at the time of the test, even though the bird may be a carrier of Psittacosis. A bird that is shedding the organism is contagious. The disease could spread to other birds or to humans at that time.

There are other methods used to test for Psittacosis, however, you may wish to consult with your veterinarian regarding how accurate these methods are, and what he or she recommends in each individual case.

Fortunately, most of the domestic birds available for purchase today are healthy and free of Psittacosis.

Psittacine Beak and Feather Testing

Many bird lovers have been caught up in a mini "hysteria" concerning African Grey Parrots contracting Psittacine Beak and Feather Disease (PBFD). Yes, African Greys can get PBFD, HOWEVER, they need to be exposed to it first! There are several methods available to test for PBFD: sending out a feather sample and the newer DNA probe test which requires a blood sample. If a bird tests positive with the DNA method, it should be retested in 90 days. I feel that the testing methods will continue to improve, but there could still be false positives.

Polyoma Virus Testing

Polyoma virus (Papovavirus) testing can be done with a swab test that can be performed on a bird or any surface the bird may come in contact with. This test is helpful for aviculturists trying to track the virus in their nursery, aviary, or incubator.

At the time of this writing, a vaccine will soon be available for adult and juvenile birds to prevent the spread of this virus. I always like to observe the data from new vaccines before I decide to vaccinate my own birds, just in case any improvements can be made.

Vaccines for Birds

There are two other vaccines available for birds: the Pox Virus vaccine, and the Pacheco's Virus vaccine. It is important to understand that both of these viruses are dangerous to birds, however they are not as common with domestic birds because these viruses used to accompany birds imported through quarantine.

Both of these vaccines come in an oil-based formula, which means it is extremely thick, and requires a fairly good-sized needle. Some birds may have a reaction to the shot, or a sore near the injection site. Cockatoos are especially sensitive to this formula. Many veterinarians do not promote these vaccines to bird owners that are not high risk in regards to being exposed to these viruses. If you work around birds or if you plan to board your bird on a regular basis, then you may wish to consider vaccinating your bird for Pacheco's Virus. The first booster consists of two shots, one month apart then one shot each year. Just like any booster shot, just because your bird is immunized does not mean your bird will have full protection; after the second booster the estimated protection is 96%.

Polyoma Virus - This vaccine is so new that at the time of this writing, it is not yet available for sale. It is in the post-production phase, and should be available soon. Polyoma Virus (formerly referred to as Papovavirus) is a deadly virus that can wipe out an entire nursery of baby psittacines before they feather out. The virus usually kills a baby bird, but an adult bird that is exposed may just become a carrier. The formula for the Polyoma Virus vaccine is not as irritating to birds, so we should see more favorable data from this vaccine. The bird should receive two boosters, one month apart, the first year, then one booster once a year thereafter.

DNA Sexing

Some African Greys are easy to visually sex, while others are not. If you are already at the veterinarian's for a routine office visit and wish to confirm the sex of your bird, you can pay for the veterinarian to take a very small sample of blood to be sent out for DNA testing to determine the gender. Two to three weeks later you will receive a certificate that confirms if your bird is male or female. This method is much less stressful than surgical sexing, which requires anesthesia.

Chapter 4

The African Grey Personality

The African Grey Personality is a very unusual one: these birds are clearly by far the best talking parrot, yet they are not always as affectionate as their owners would like them to be! African Grey parrots have a broad tone range, so it enables them to be able to mimic just about any sound they like, and they are also able to speak in more than one tone of voice.

Some African Greys will let their owners pet or cuddle with them, but most act indifferent to physical touch; others would rather not be touched, and will let you know. I wish I could say that all you need to do is socialize these birds when they are young, and get them used to all sorts of petting, and handling; unfortunately, you can do this and your grey may still have a different opinion on this matter, although it doesn't hurt to try!

Male African Greys seem to favor the woman of the household, and female African Greys love attention from the man of the house. Even if another person hand-feeds the bird while it is young, this seems to almost always stand true.

African Greys are extremely intelligent birds, and they seem to understand and absorb more of the household stress that affects us on a day to day basis. I truly believe this is why African Greys have a reputation for feather plucking. From the time we wake up in the morning until the time we go to bed, we are in a state of trying to coordinate all of our daily chores, work, and relaxation, if there's any time for that. Our birds are very perceptive to our moods, and I am sure that the African Grey is exceptionally so. I also feel that part of their frustration is their inability to relieve tension. As humans, we have many ways to relieve tension: exercise, get out of the house for a concert or movie, go shopping, or get together with friends. What can our birds do? Not much more than chew their feathers, scream, or bite. It is very helpful to take your bird out of the house, and expose it to outside changes, other people, and sometimes other birds. Your bird may be very frightened, but with gradual exposure, he or she may even learn to like getting out of the house.

The Typical African Grey

Most African Greys form a close bond with one person in the immediate family, or just the family members.

African Greys do not necessarily enjoy being petted, and if they do, it is usually on their terms. Nancy Richetts has a West African Grey named Rosie that lets her pet it on occasion. Sue Ballmer has a Congo named Casey that lets her pet him almost any time. Deborah Fielder has a Timneh, Scooter, that also likes petting.

African Greys have a devilish side to their personality, also. Many of my customers have told me how their African Greys know their dogs by name, and love to call the dogs in the owner's voice, only to laugh at them when they come running!

Most Greys are very aware of all family members in a household, and will identify and call each family member by the correct name. This is pretty amazing, because most other parrots are not as likely to be as accurate or concerned with association.

Greys are definitely creatures of habit, and they do not like changes in their environment (that doesn't mean there shouldn't be any, but sometimes a gradual change is better if it is possible). Most greys do not like water or bathing, more will be said about this in Chapter 7. When purchasing toys, most of my customers will select toys that are smaller and less intimidating to their birds.

If there are other pets in the household, almost all of my survey recipients replied that their greys did not like them, or they tolerated them. While some greys were afraid of cats, others liked them. Nancy Richetts also mentioned that they have two cats with different meows, and that their grey, Rosie, will meow appropriately to each cat!

I think the person who summed it up the best about her three (yes, 3!) African Greys was my friend Diana Craven:

"The greys are absolutely, incredibly intelligent and intuitive. I am constantly amazed by the things they do and the intelligence they display in my day-to-day interaction with them. They will kiss me, then lower their heads for kisses. Sabrina knows that when I have finished showering with Lulu (Diana's pet Yellow-Naped Amazon), it is her turn to come into the bathroom with me while I dry my hair. She says, 'Good night' when I turn off the television at night; never during the day. Pingo will tell Lulu to 'knock it off' when she goes on one of her crying jags. These aren't tricks; the birds are just plain smart and know much more than I ever dreamt a bird could know. I love all my birds, but if I could only keep one, it would be a Grey."

Other Grey Personalities

Ray Oban lives in a small town with wife and his nine year old Congo African grey, Katie. He wrote, "Katie is a regular at the bank, hardware store, and lumber yard. She likes people and I hold her for children to pet. She's pretty calm about it. She'll show her wings, lay on her back and say, 'Hello' or whistle for the dog. She likes bike rides, she sings and whistles on our morning walks. If my wife and her dog are along, she is quiet. When she hears a dog bark she will answer with her bark."

African greys do seem to be very in tune with the family dog(s), and my friend Marjorie Powell wrote about Whidbey, her 16 year-old African grey: "Whidbey knows all four dogs names. One night about 9:30 p.m. I hadn't covered his cage. I was reading and all was quiet when suddenly Whidbey said, 'Do you want to go outside Nib?' (Nib is one of the four dogs) With that I heard Nib woof at the door to get out."

Diane Gallagher travels in her motor home with Niaya, her 3 year old Congo African Grey. In November 1994, Diane's mother died, and Diane took Niaya with her to Oregon. Diane wrote: "I was doing an estate sale and was having a particularly emotional day. I walked in my motorhome crying and Niaya looked at me and in the softest most welcoming tone said, 'Hi, Darlin'. It was just what I needed to hear. I did not feel as alone with her there. Having Niaya is like having another person around because she is very sensitive to my moods and needs."

Niaya likes to travel and her foot muscles are strong from riding on her travel perch. Photo by Diane Gallagher.

My friend and well-known bird breeder Gail Worth owns an 8 year-old female Congo African grey named Togo. She hatched and hand-raised the bird as a present for her husband, Dave, and the bird has become a talented addition to their household. Togo started talking around the usual age of one year, and now will learn a new phrase in one weekend. Gail will repeat the phrase every time she passes by the cage starting on Friday, and by Monday (if her bird likes the new phrase) Togo will have mastered it. Here are a few of the things that Togo likes to say:

"Give that bird a beer!"
"No Budweiser for me/I only drink pale ale!"
"I want a hot pot pie"
"Close, but no Cigar"
"Better get cash!"
"I'll get you my pretty, and your little dog, too!"
"Ride that Harley Hog, Dave!"
"I'll get you my fat rat and your Harley hog, too!"
"Don't stare at me you ninny!"
"Your face looks like a cow pie"

One trait that is very common for African greys to do when they talk is to combine or mix up phrases to what the bird likes to say. Gail added a third dimension to speech training Togo when she made exaggerated mannerisms, and the bird copied them. Here are two examples: (1) Gail taught Togo to say, "I dress in Corinthian feathers" and at the same time, she (Gail) held her arms out and moved them gracefully up and down. When the bird learned this phrase, she also moved her wings gracefully up and down and struts everytime she says it; (2) Gail would point at Togo and exclaim, "You, you, you!" and "You look like a fuddy duddy!" and Togo learned these phrases with an added twist-she lifts her right foot and "points" her toe when she says it.

Finally, who says greys have to be tame to have personality? Gail has several wild pairs set up for breeding in the backyard of her home that started a "game" with her (it actually started with one bird and now they all seem to "play"). The game goes like this: Gail will go outside and yell towards the grey's cages, "Does anybody have any eggs? And one grey will answer, "No!" Then she will ask, "How about later this week?" another will answer, "Nooo!" then she will ask, "Later this month?" again, "Nooo!" Then she will ask "Anytime later this year?" and a final grey will answer emphatically, "Nooooo!"

Chapter 5

Diet and Vitamins

There is still little known about what the perfect diet is for any of the psittacine birds, much less specifically the African Grey. The pelleted diets are bombarding the market with claims that their formulas are complete, and no additional foodstuffs are needed, but I have reservations about second-guessing just what our precious birds need to live a long, healthy, disease-free life.

If we don't know exactly what our bird's nutritional needs are, then I believe that it is best that we try to offer them a large variety of food items, in hopes that we will possibly meet whatever specific dietary needs they have. Unfortunately, birds are like small children, and they do not always want to eat everything we want them to. In this case, some skillful techniques will need to be tried to get finicky birds to eat a more healthy diet. Let's start with what to offer the "bird that will eat everything" and go from there:

It is easiest to feed your bird with three feed bowls: one for seeds and nuts, one for fruits and vegetables, and one for fresh water everyday. (I like to have an extra set of feed bowls so that I can simply swap a dirty bowl for a clean one, and there is less time involved in feeding.)

I feed our African Greys a large-hookbill seed mixture that offers a variety of seeds and other ingredients: safflower seeds, rolled corn, pistachio nuts, banana chips, raw almonds and walnuts, pine nuts, kibble corn, buckwheat, hemp, and some pellets. Sunflower seeds are okay if they are not a large portion of the mixture. Many years ago a rumor was started that sunflower seeds contained narcotic qualities, and that the birds became addicted to them. This theory, however was proved to be untrue (from actual tests) but the rumor lingers on. The latest information that is important is the fact that sunflower seeds are high in fat-many people have switched their birds to a safflower based seed mixture thinking that these seeds are lower in fat, when in fact the safflower seeds are just as fattening! Your best goal is to find a seed mixture that features many different seeds, or buy several different types of seed blends and mix them together. In the survey, almost every bird owner reported that their birds loved safflower seeds the best. This is interesting, because safflower seeds are very bitter, and parrots don't have many taste buds, so they may be attracted to their strong flavor for this reason.

African Grey parrots are usually very efficient eaters, and devour everything in their seed bowls. I also believe that they have a high metabolism rate, because I rarely see an overweight African Grey.

The fruit and vegetable bowl should vary slightly every day, to prevent your birds from getting bored with the same menu, and to get them used to new things in their bowl. Here is a list of fruits and vegetables that you can try serving your African Grey:

Apples, oranges, grapes, pears, peaches and nectarines (without the pits), blueberries, raspberries, strawberries, bananas, kiwi fruit, cantaloupe, honeydew, watermelon, plums (without the pits), sweet potatoes, yams, red/yellow/green peppers, chili peppers, broccoli, Brussels sprouts, carrots, beets & their tops, tomatoes, alfalfa sprouts, squash, bok choy, spinach and green beans. Just be sure that you do not feed Brussels sprouts or spinach more than once or twice a week, because they contain Oxalic acid, which interferes with calcium absorption; they still have many nutrients, so it is not harmful to feed these items.

You should serve your African Grey fresh fruits and vegetables every day.

There is still much controversy over whether Avocado is harmful to birds; I truly believe it is, even though I am not sure why. I had two customers whose Cockatiels died after eating avocado, and I do not believe it is worth taking the chance. Some people believe that avocado is very high in fat, and that is why the birds react to it, I have also heard that the meat next to the pit is harmful; for now it is best to avoid this fruit altogether.

In addition to the fruit and vegetable arrangement, I like to serve my greys small cut-up pieces of wheat bread, unsalted crackers, rice cakes (plain or flavored varieties) crackers, pellets or dog kibble.

Table Food

Unless you are a junk-food junkie, you should encourage your African Grey to eat healthy table food. The advantage to this is preventing your bird from becoming a finicky eater, and offering a well-rounded diet.

Offer your grey anything that is not too greasy, spicy, or high in fat. Steamed or cooked vegetables are excellent, and breads and pasta are also good. You may give your grey any meat that is thoroughly cooked, and with the bone. For example, if you give your grey a rib bone with some meat on it, your bird may crack the bone open and eat the marrow inside. Birds are not like dogs, and they will not swallow bone fragments, they will, however, drop bone pieces onto the ground, so use caution if you have a dog. (Chicken bones can be harmful to dogs because they may splinter and if the dog eats a piece of bone with a sharp edge, it may cause serious harm to the dog's digestive organs.) Also be sure that you do not eat the meat off of the bone, and then hand the bone to the bird; your saliva could possibly make the bird ill.

Vegetarians can offer their birds cooked beans and legumes, which are great protein for birds. Breakfast cereal with milk, yogurt and ice cream are all okay, as long as dairy products do not make up more than 10% of the bird's total diet, because birds cannot digest lactose in milk.

An occasional potato chip or cookie won't hurt your bird, but don't let the bird binge on junk food, because it is not healthy. Also limit caffeine in the form of coffee, tea, and sodas. Alcohol is extremely dangerous for any bird, in any quantity.

Note: Do not feed your bird chocolate, it may be toxic to your bird.

Amost every single pet grey in the survey eats some type of table food, the favorites were: Chicken and chicken bones, pizza, pasta, eggs, hard-boiled eggs, scrambled eggs, tuna salad, yogurt, ice cream, mashed potatoes, baked potatoes, spaghetti noodles, pork chops, cheese, and steak.

Pellets

Pelleted diets come in many different flavors, colors and textures. We add a small percentage (about 5%) to our seed mixture and we sometimes add pellets to the fruit and vegetable bowl.

It is very tempting to only have to buy one thing at the bird store, however, there is just not enough data available to substantiate that pellets are more healthy on a long-term basis. There is so much competition in the pet food industry that there are many different types of pellets available for bird owners to choose from.

I believe that birds are very limited in their activities. Stirring through their seeds and picking out their favorites and discarding their least favorite items gives them something to do. We have to remember that in the wild, birds may not eat a wide variety of food items (some do, some don't), but the time and energy expended to get to those food items is a large part of their daily routine. If we serve our birds one dish with one food item, it's extremely boring for the bird.

It is also important to change pellets daily as they will become stale. Look for a brand of pellets that has a "use-by" date on it, so you can be assured of its freshness.

We have already seen and we will continue to see many improvements in the development of pelleted diets in the future.

Vitamins

It is important to understand that if your bird eats a very well-rounded diet, lots of fruits and vegetables, and some healthy table food, vitamins are probably not necessary. Unfortunately, most birds are picky to some degree, so vitamin supplementation is recommended. We prefer to use a powdered vitamin supplement such as Avia®, Super Preen®, or Nekton-S®, that contains vitamins, minerals, and amino acids to sprinkle on the seeds or fruits and vegetables. We may use this vitamin two or three times a week.

Calcium

It has been the belief that African Grey Parrots are more prone to calcium deficiencies, more so than other psittacines, however, some aviculturists believe that this is not true. Until we hear otherwise, however, we like to supplement our grey's calcium levels, and if anything, it may strengthen their bones so that in the event they injure themselves (African Greys are known for being clumsy) they may heal easier!

There are many different types of Calcium supplements available, the most commonly used brands are: D-Ca-Fos® and Neo-Calglucon®. D-Ca-Fos® is a white powder that is sprinkled on the seed or fruit. Most veterinarians recommend 1/8 teaspoon several times a week, unless the bird has a confirmed calcium deficiency, then it may be more. Neo-Calglucon® is available through most pharmacies (without a prescription), and is a syrup that is added to the water. There is no set dosage on the Neo-Calglucon®, we use 1 teaspoon in a 12-ounce crock of water; most veterinarians will recommend 3cc's per 4 ounces of water.

There is also a good calcium source in cuttlebone, so don't hesitate to buy your African Grey a cuttlebone if he or she will eat it. Mineral Blocks have smaller amounts of calcium, however they are good for alleviating boredom, and some birds like them.

Water

We serve our birds fresh tap water every day in a clean bowl. When using tap water, let the water run freely for about five minutes before filling your birds' water bowls. This should rid the water of any possible contaminants that may have settled in the pipes. It is not desirable to use water from a hose, but if you have no choice, let the water run 15 minutes to avoid contaminants in your water.

You may serve your birds bottled water if you like, but be aware that not all bottled water is as pure as it claims to be. If you use a dispenser for your bottled water, clean the entire unit with bleach and water once a week to avoid contaminating your water with a dirty dispenser.

There are many different types of water filtration systems, some are more efficient that others, and some filter out bacteria and viruses better. A system with an ultraviolet section is a good choice because ultraviolet kills germs and bacteria.

Chapter 6

Cages, Perches, Playstands and Toys

Gone are the days when a pet bird is kept in a tiny cage without any toys. Pet product manufacturers are stumbling over each other to market a large selection of cages, perches and toys. Buying a bird cage is like buying a new car; how many features do you want, and how much are you willing to pay?

The Ideal Cage

The ideal cage for an African Grey is at least 24" wide x 24" deep, x 30" tall (actual cage section, not including stand, and wheels). Bigger still is better, if you have room available; I know of many very happy African greys that live in cages that are 34 or 36 inches wide. The spacing between the bars should be less than $1^1/4$ inches for Congos and Ghanas, and less than $1^1/16$" for Timnehs, so they cannot get their head stuck. Wrought-iron (actually cold-rolled steel) cages are now available in an assortment of colors. If your grey likes to chip at the paint on the cage, try to purchase a cage that is sandblasted before painting, because the paint will last longer. If you have a chip on a new cage when you purchase it, make sure you can't continue to peel it, or your bird will do the same. (You may touch up your bird's cage with household spray paint; just be sure that the label says, "Safe for Children's Furniture-Lead Free" and that the paint is allowed to dry before placing the bird back into the cage.) If you never want to worry about normal paint wear and tear, then you may want to invest in a stainless steel cage, which is more costly.

The most versatile choice is a cage that is on wheels, with a playpen on the top. When you are home, you can open the door to the cage and the bird can play on top; when you need to go to work, or at night, the bird can be securely locked inside. (It is not recommended to leave your grey outside of its cage when you are not home, because it could become frightened, fly off the cage and injure itself, or chew on an electrical cord or another dangerous household item.)

Dome top cages are more roomy and offer your bird a high-up hideaway inside of the cage. Many people with cages in one room and play trees in another opt for the dome top to give their birds the extra space.

It is good to have at least 3 bowl holders in your cage, if the cage only comes with 2, then you can add an extra holder and feed bowl. This way you can serve seeds and nuts in one, fruits and vegetables in another, and water in the third bowl.

This Neon Cockatoo Adventure cage is an ideal home for Benjamin, who likes the extra room to climb around, and play with toys.

The newer cages now feature aprons around the bottom, which facilitates cleaning, and catches food items that are dropped or thrown. Another advantage of having an apron around the cage is when the bird sits on the edge or corner of the cage, it cannot "poop on the carpet".

Pat Naymola has a macaw-sized cage for her Timneh Grey, Smokey, and she says he is much happier in a big cage.

Perches

The perches inside of your grey's cage should be natural wood. Avoid manzanita wood perches, because it is very slippery, and your grey will not feel comfortable on such a slick surface.

Ribbon wood, eucalyptus, maple, pine, oak, and branches from fruit trees are all fine; if you cut down a branch from a tree, be sure it has not been sprayed with any pesticides that might make your bird ill. Rinse off any branches with disinfectant and let them dry in the sun before putting them inside of your grey's cage.

Congos should have perches approximately 1 to $1^1/2$ inches in diameter, and Ghanas and Timnehs should have perches 3/4 to 1 inch in diameter. It is good to have a variety of perches in your bird's cage, and not all the same width.

The new bolt-on cement perches are wonderful for all birds because they wear down the tips of the nails, and are not abrasive to the bird's feet. These sometimes come in bright colors that the birds do not like, so you may have to introduce one of these slowly. An older grey may really be distressed at the sight of the perch, and sometimes it is just not worth stressing the bird. Birds like to rub their beaks on these perches, which is fine, as long as it is not excessively rubbing the top layer of the beak off.

Playstands

I think it is important to realize the importance of giving our pet birds mobility inside and outside the home, so they don't become bored as easily. Having a mobile playstand is handy and good for all pet birds to have a break from their cage. If you are going to work or play outside, and your bird's wings are trimmed, then you can take the bird outside to get some sun. Be careful if there are birds of prey; they have been known to swoop down on pet birds that are easy targets.

A playstand can be a simple T-stand with food and water, or it can be an elaborate tree with toys, swings, and ladders attached.

Most of the greys in the survey had playstands in addition to their cages, and when their owners are home, they are allowed to be out on their playstand. Noreen Cooper has a Congo named Simba that has three playpens, and she says he uses all of them!

Important Note: Always keep natural wood perches and stands clean and free from fecal matter; clean the perch with a disinfectant, or hose it off and scrub with soap and water periodically. You may wish to use a stiff scrub brush to remove dried fecal matter.

Natural wood playstands provide a place for African Greys to play, chew and destroy, or just hang out. The more levels and toys, the better.

Toys

It is important to introduce a lot of different sizes, shapes and colors of toys if you have a new baby grey. If your bird is older, chances are he or she does not always like new toys, and you may have to slowly introduce anything new.

Always check toys for safety features before buying them. Look for welded chains, quick-link fasteners (birds love to undo keyring fasteners, however, after undoing a toy over and over, the bird can get a groove in it's beak from the keyring, or even worse, get hung up on their beak on the keyring), un-tanned leather, wood blocks dyed with food coloring or jello, and pieces of rope that are not too long, and that can be trimmed or removed once the bird has shredded it.

These are the favorite toys of birds in the survey: the cardboard tube from paper towel rolls, paper to shred, soft rope toys, hand-held plastic toys, anything hanging that features rope, wood, and leather, acrylic toys, squeaky dog toys, soft wood toys that shred easily, leather strips tied in knots, and the all-around favorite: bells. Look for a bell that is well-made and one that the clapper cannot be easily removed; some of the large copper bells are long lasting with curious parrots that love to immediately remove the clapper.

Most African Greys love to play with bells.

Since African Greys are so smart, I thought it would also be interesting to find out what colors the birds liked, if the owner saw a preference, and what colors they were afraid of. Some owners did not know, while others mentioned that their greys liked the following colors: Orange, red, fushia, yellow, blue, purple and dark colors. Those who noticed their birds were afraid of certain colors mentioned yellow, white, and bright colors, or bright colors and patterns.

I also strongly feel that every bird, greys especially, should have a swing. My friend Darlene Fitchet has a Congo grey named Barkley (after the famous Phoenix Suns basketball player, Charles Barkley) that loves his swing. I realized how important this toy was to the bird when I spent a few days at Darlene's home, observing her grey, and trying to teach it new phrases. Think about a rocking chair for us: if you sit in one, it is very therapeutic to want to rock yourself while you are sitting in the chair. The swing has two benefits: it is a mild form of exercise, and it has a calming affect. I think every grey should have one!

One fun activity to do with your bird is to bring it with you to the bird store to "pick out" a toy. It's lots of fun to hold two toys in front of a bird and ask it which one it likes-it will almost always lean over to touch the one it likes. (Please do not let your bird chew on any toys that you do not intend to buy-the store owners or nearby customers may not appreciate it!)

Some African Greys love to take a bath, like Clouseau, while others shiver at the thought! Photo by Cyndi Peirce.

Lexi prefers her bath outside, with a garden hose! Photo by Cort Vallens.

Chapter 7

Bathing and Grooming

It is amazing that even though the Congos and the Ghanas are from a very lush area of the rainforests in Africa, in captivity the majority of them hate bathing. Greys have been seen in their native habitat flying daily in rain, unlike other parrots.

The most important thing to do is to introduce a young bird to bathing, misting, and towels as soon as it is weaned, and to be consistent, so the bird does not develop a fear of being bathed. It's okay if the bird doesn't really like to be misted or bathed, as long as it understands that this ritual is going to occur whether it likes it or not. It sometimes helps if you give your bird a pine nut or other treat everytime you finish misting or bathing it, as a "reward".

There are several ways to bathe your grey, the easiest is to take it into the shower with you. You may also mist your grey with a spray bottle, or you can fill the sink or tub with an inch of water and let the bird splash around.

Important Note: Anytime you are in the bathroom with your bird, always securely close the lid to the toilet, in case your bird should become frightened and jump inside. Birds have drowned before in the bathroom!

If your bird is afraid of bathing, the best thing to do is to just take it into the bathroom while you take a shower. Put your grey on the shower curtain rod and talk to it while you bathe. After a week or two of just watching, next take your grey and very quickly run it under the very outside edge of the water and put it back on the shower curtain rod. Each time after this, try to get your grey more and more used to the water, and hold it under the water for longer periods of time. Hopefully, your bird will become somewhat desensitized from its water phobia and you will be able to bathe it.

The more often you bathe your grey the better its feathers will look. The average grey owner bathes their bird once a week, and some of the survey respondents said that when their grey was ready for a bath (they would show signs, like jumping in the water dish) they would go ahead and bathe their bird.

Because African Greys and Cockatoos have a protective dusty coating on their feathers, it is extremely important that you do not bathe your grey with a general, all-purpose bird bath spray, because most of these contain a synthetic oil, which is okay for South American birds, but not for greys or cockatoos. Water is fine. If your bird is extremely dirty, you may use Cockatoo or Parrot Shampoo, first soak the bird thoroughly with water, then apply a small amount of Cockatoo or Parrot Shampoo, then rinse the bird very well.

Grooming

I have groomed many African Grey parrots and I believe that the key to successful, low-stress bird grooming is: taking a minute to "talk" to the bird, confidently catching the bird in a towel, and working quickly (less than 5 minutes) and praising the bird when you are done. When I "talk" to the bird, I always ask the owner the bird's name, and then I set the bird in a corner on a low perch. I say hello to the bird, and tell it I am going to groom it, and that I will do it as quickly as I can, and that I will not hurt it. Animals know or sense most of our intentions, and I believe that this approach has helped immensely with grooming the African Greys, because they do not like it one bit!

Many African Greys will hold a grudge against their owners if they groom the bird themselves; I have found that if the owner started grooming the bird when it was very young, it is not usually a problem. It is when a grey owner "decides" to start grooming their own bird after its older that sometimes the bird will turn against the owner, either for a short period of time, and sometimes longer. It helps to reward the bird with a favorite nut, or a small chew toy after each time you groom it, and praise the bird so it will learn to associate a treat after each time it is groomed. If you are learning how to groom and you cannot do all of the nails and wings in less than 5 minutes, then you need to break up the grooming into two or three sessions, at least a few days apart. There is nothing more stressful to your bird than being wrapped in a towel for longer than 5 minutes, and your bird is less likely to hate you if you do not restrain it for long periods of time. If your bird needs special filing to its beak, and you are not sure how to file it, find someone with experience to show you the first time.

Most veterinarians will groom birds, and a very small percentage use isoflorane to briefly sedate the bird so they can groom it. I personally think this is an unneccessary stress to the bird (any time a bird is given anesthesia, you have a slight risk to its life).

The only time this may be necessary is if there is an impacted feather, or feather follicle, and the veterinarian feels it would be better to sedate the bird. If you are lucky enough to find an experienced bird groomer, most are used to the wildest macaw and the tiniest canary.

African Greys should have their toenails trimmed and their wings trimmed approximately every 12 weeks. African Greys should be trimmed differently than other large hookbills because they are not as graceful and are accident prone if their wings or nails are trimmed too short.

Nails

Toenails on an African Grey can get very sharp on the ends, but they are rarely very long. The ends should be filed with a Dremel® tool, or carefully clipped with dog nail clippers or cat claw scissors. Always have styptic powder nearby when you trim nails in case a nail starts to bleed. If this does happen, pack the nail with styptic powder to stop the bleeding. If you do not have any styptic powder, you may use flour, cornstarch, or talcum powder, however, styptic powder has a chemical cauterizer that stops bleeding more efficiently.

Here's the proper amount to trim on the African Grey's toenails:

It is extremely important to hold the bird's toe and nail firmly; if you only grip the nail, the bird may move suddenly and break the toe, or tear the nail off the toe. (It's not very common, but it does happen.)

African Greys have a very tight grip, so use care when trying to extend the foot for grooming; if you pull too hard, you may break the toe. The best way to get the bird to loosen its grip is to tickle the bird's foot, or to start dremeling the very tip of the toenail and the vibration will stimulate the bird to open its grip. Another technique is to let go of the foot, and try for a better hold.

Wings

African Greys should have 5-7 primary flight feathers clipped. If the bird is a very strong flyer, then you may clip 9 feathers, but 7 is usually adequate. Be sure you clip underneath the covert feathers to avoid hitting a blood feather. If you clip the wings correctly, you will never experience a bleeding feather! See below:

Clip 5-7 flight feathers, and be sure to cut below the covert feathers. Strong flyers may need 7-9 feathers cut.

Important Note: Proper holding technique is essential! If you are not sure how to hold your grey for grooming or inspection, then it is very important that you learn how. Do not chase your bird around the house trying to catch it in a towel, instead, take it to the bathtub or put it in a corner and use a large bath towel so you can catch it up on the first try. When you chase a bird around, it becomes stressed, and its heart rate increases; if you trim a nail too short, it is likely to bleed because the bird is worked up.

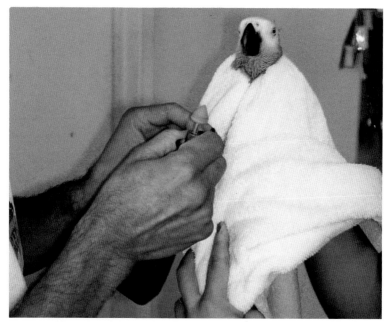

The proper way to hold a grey with two people.

The proper position when grooming by yourself.

Beaks

Many African Grey owners think that the white lines on their bird's beaks are cracks. These lines really indicate a build-up of keratin, the material their beak is made of. Because in captivity our birds do not get the chance to fly around, gnaw on tree branches, and rub their beaks on rocks, they experience a build-up on their beak. These ridges are not harmful unless they become quite thick, and at that point, it becomes a stress-point, and if the bird was to fall abruptly on a hard surface, the beak could break at that line. To avoid this type of injury, most groomers will file the beak (usually by hand with a professional manicurist's nail file-medium coarseness), and file down the excess keratin so the beak is smooth, and even on both sides. Occasionally a grey will have a problem with its beak growing longer or thicker on one side; it is not known for certain what causes this, however, it is something that requires regular grooming, so the beak does not become crooked, or the bird unable to eat.

The upper mandible of an African Grey may become too long; if this happens, the best thing to do is to file the tip of the beak by hand with a over-sized professional manicurist's nail file. You should buy a file (the black ones work the best) that is medium in courseness. Always file in one direction when working on the tip of the beak; this is so you do not exert unnecessary stress with back and forth strokes on the tip, which can be somewhat sensitive. If you are buffing out ridges on top of the beak, it is okay to use a back and forth motion.

If you do your own grooming, be sure to disinfect your equipment after each time you use it. Don't forget to spray disinfectant on the dremel tip, nail files, scissors, and any other tools used.

Chapter 8

Boarding Your Grey

Whether you travel for business, or just want to take a family vacation, the situation may arise when you need to board your African Grey. Many bird people also have dogs, cats, and other pets, and will often pay someone to stay in their home and care for their animals. If this is an option, by all means you should do it. However, most people do not know individuals that are familiar with birds, and do not have this option available to them. In this case, it is necessary to find a person or a shop that can board your bird for you.

The whole boarding experience is usually more stressful on the bird owner than on the bird itself! Most birds adapt quite well, and some look forward to a change in their routine.

Here are a few things to consider when choosing a reputable boarding place for your bird:

- Is the bird area clean?
- Do the employees know how to handle birds?
- Are there any health requirements?
- Do they feed fruits and vegetables?
- Are they equipped to transfer your bird to a
  veterinarian if emergency medical care is necessary?
- Would you feel comfortable leaving your bird there?
- Is the location secure enough (i.e., alarm, gates or dogs).
- Does the boarding facility feed the same diet as you do? or,
- Are you allowed to bring your own diet for your bird?

Most boarding facilities will have you sign a boarding contract that gives them permission to seek veterinary attention for your bird if it should become ill (all veterinarian fees are your responsibility). You should also list a telephone number where you can be reached in case of emergency (if one is available). The boarding contract should also specify if the bird will be replaced in the event of fire or theft. Finally, if another member of your family, or a friend is going to pick up your bird you should note it on the contract, because most places will not release the bird to someone else without prior consent of the owner.

When you board your bird in a store, it is important to understand that there are some health risks involved. Your bird will be exposed to other birds, and that is why it is important that you feel comfortable with the cleanliness and general health of the birds that are kept in the store. If you wish to have your bird checked by a veterinarian after it is boarded, then it is best to wait at least one week after you pick the bird up. The reason for this is so that if your bird was exposed to something like a virus that has an incubation period, it will not show up on any tests right away, and you are more likely to get more accurate test results if you wait. (Of course, if your bird doesn't look right, go to your vet right away.)

How do the African Greys handle being boarded? We have boarded many African Greys at our store and the ones that do the best are the ones that come in often (more than 4 times a year). These birds like coming in, and they have already figured out that their owner will be back for them each time. It is important to "tell" your bird when you are are leaving it, and that you will be back. It may not understand what you are saying, but the tone of your voice will be reassuring to it, and it does help.

Important Note: If you take your bird to be boarded and it also is due for wings, nails and beak grooming, do NOT have the bird groomed when it arrives at the boarding facility, or it will be extremely unhappy from its stressful introduction to the new place. Try to have the bird groomed one to two weeks before you take it to be boarded, or have the bird groomed the same day you pick it up. The only exception to this is if your bird's wings have suddenly grown out, and you fear the bird may be able to fly away; then just have the wings clipped, and save the nails and beak for later.

If you take one or two of your bird's favorite toys with you when you board it, it may feel more comfortable. Some birds are comforted with a swing. Others like to be in a tall, or high cage. Others don't seem to care. Some greys prefer being around people, while others may enjoy a quieter area. You may wish to let the boarding facility know your bird's personality traits, so they can make it as comfortable as possible.

If your bird is on a special diet, then you had better make sure that the boarding facility you choose will be able to accomodate you. It is extra work for a store to feed one particular bird a completely different diet, and some stores will not be able to do this for you.

Avoid cooked food items, because they spoil very quickly and you will not be there to pick up your bird's leftovers, and it is asking a lot to expect someone else to do so. Many bird owners understand that their birds will not be eating the same diet as in the home, and as long as it is similar, that should be sufficient.

African Greys love to listen to the noises of a new place, and after you bring your bird home, it will probably mimic every bird and sound it heard. Some greys are extremely noisy when they come home, and this usually takes about one week for the noise level to taper down. If your grey was caged next to another grey, it may have either taught the other bird something new, or picked up something the other bird said!

If your bird does not pick its feathers, chances are it will not begin to do so if you leave it with someone. I know of several birds that did start picking their feathers, however, with people who went away for the weekend, and left extra food and water and just left the bird "home alone." Not only is this bad for the bird physically, but it is extremely stressful emotionally for the bird. Birds feel abandoned when their owners do not come home when they are supposed to, and when it happens, the results are usually disastrous. Even if you have to pay someone to come over to your home to feed and water the bird, and turn on lights, television, etc., it is better than leaving the bird by itself.

Birds that already pick their feathers will usually continue to do so when they are boarded. It is a compulsive behavior by this time, and there is not much you can do about it. If your bird likes to chew on paper, leather, or wood chunks, leave extra for the bird to demolish while you are gone.

Some African Greys actually look forward to being boarded!

African Greys are stimulated by change, and you may be pleasantly surprised when you pick up your grey after your vacation. Our store recently boarded a grey that visited for $2^1/2$ weeks while its owner went to visit relatives out of the country. This bird was rarely away from its owner, and the first few days this bird was so scared, it practically hugged its perch, and flapped its wings nervously. I would go by the cage and talk to it, and I could tell by its eyes that it was stressed. (When greys are stressed, their eyes are opened very wide, and the pupil is not really dilated or constricted, it's just sort of "frozen" in a wide-eyed position.) I would always talk to the bird, and try to reassure it. The owner had told us that the bird talked a lot, and could count to four. After about 3 days, I put a toy inside of the cage to see if that would distract the bird, but he was not interested. After being in the store for a few more days, I noticed that the bird seemed more relaxed; he played with the toy I had given him, and he was talking. I heard him counting and decided to try to teach him to count up to 5. After about 2 days, he was counting up to five! By this time he was very content, and enjoyed being in a new place. I really like to see birds make this turnaround, because I believe it helps them, and they become better birds because of it.

Sometimes when there are lots of larger birds screaming in our store one of the boarding birds (usually a Macaw or African Grey) will yell, "Quiet!".

It is good to aquaint your African Grey with the place you are going to board him before the actual date arrives. I encourage customers to bring in their bird for a "visit" (no grooming, just socializing) before they drop them off for boarding.

It is not right to skip your vacation because you are worried about your bird(s). While you are away, don't hesitate to call periodically to see how your bird is doing if it will make you feel better. Not only will the change be good, but you might enjoy yourself, too!

Chapter 9

What Frightens Greys

African Grey parrots are creatures of habit, and when something new appears in their environment, they are likely to become frightened. If you introduce new things into the home slowly, or with an explanation, your grey will adapt more easily. You can stop feather picking in its early stages if you know something is frightening your grey and you remove the scary thing from the environment as soon as possible.

In, On and Around the Cage

Any new perches, toys, swings, perches, or a new cage may frighten some African Greys. The best way to acclimate your grey to a new toy is to put the toy on a table near the cage, and each time you go by your grey's cage, pick up the toy, show it to the bird, and tell the bird how much it will like playing with this toy. You want to try to interest the bird, but continue to leave the toy out of the cage for a few days. Once you feel the bird is comfortable with the toy inside of its cage, go ahead and put it inside.

Perches or playpens are large, bulky and scary to some birds, so it is best if you can put the perch inside of the house across the room from your grey's cage. Gradually move the perch closer to the grey's location, and show your bird all of the moving parts and features of the new perch. Do not put your grey on the perch unless you know it is not afraid of it, otherwise it will jump off, head straight for the floor, and it may injure itself.

New cages are also better accepted if they are not switched immediately for the old one. Place the new cage near the bird's location, and move a few of your bird's old, familiar toys inside of it. Put food and water inside the cage, and keep the two cages side by side for a few days. When you feel your bird will accept the new cage, go ahead and take out the old one.

Occasionally you will buy a new toy or other item that your Grey just does not seem to accept; in this case I would recommend you do not try to pursue convincing your grey this new toy is okay; maybe something similar in a different color may be sufficient.

There were many interesting comments from our grey surveys as to what greys are afraid of:

Casey, a Congo African Grey owned by Debbie Schnieder, is afraid of large objects brought past her cage, like a large trash can or box. She especially hates the dolly Debbie uses to haul the trash out.

Chris Mills wrote that his Congo hates the stuffed animals his wife has arranged on the couch; especially the stuffed bear and lion.

Veradel Ballard has a Congo named Willie that is afraid of the color red, and of the vacuum cleaner. (Many other grey owners replied that their birds were afraid of the vacuum.)

Moe, a Congo African Grey owned by Jennifer Hill is afraid of earthquakes. (This is a fear of all pet birds.)

Homer, a Congo owned by Cary Asuncion, is afraid of golf clubs, white washcloths and towels.

Here are some other items that Greys were afraid of:

Towels
Brooms
Neckties
Bread Machine Noises
Anything Yellow
Anything White
Ironing Boards
People in Hats
Ceiling Fans
Children
Cats
Loud Noises
Water

The most common thing Greys were fearful of was new or large objects.

Chapter 10

Speech Training

If you purchase a hand-fed African Grey you may start speech training it right away, but these birds normally do not begin to talk until they are around one year old. I like to call this the "sponge" stage, because they are absorbing every sound, whistle, and word that you say, but they have not yet mastered the art of repeating much of anything. Most African Greys start to whistle or imitate noises that they hear in the home before they start to talk. Greys are natural born whistlers, and whistling is part of their natural calls and noises they make. It is a myth that if you teach a bird to whistle it will not learn to talk.

I have seen a few young African Greys (around 10-14 weeks old) that were trying to talk, and heard a very squeaky "hello" or "hi". Typically, most baby greys make cute little puppy noises, or whine for attention, and then later they imitate a telephone ring, or a microwave beep, a door squeak, or an answering machine "beep". Right around 6-8 months, a baby grey may say a few simple words or short phrases. Or it may say nothing at all. By the time the bird is one year old it will usually start saying new words on a regular basis. Some greys are late bloomers and don't repeat very many words or phrases until they are $1^1/2$ to 2 years of age. Normally, around 2 years old, you have to be careful what you say around them, because they are more than likely to repeat anything they hear. I have never seen a hand-fed African Grey that didn't eventually learn to talk. Of course, some greys seem to really catch on quickly and learn new things, while others seem to be stuck on a few phrases. I believe a lot of this has to do with the environment, and the initiative of the bird's owner.

Important Note: Wild-caught African greys can also be excellent talkers; it usually takes them at least a year to feel comfortable enough to start talking.

I have a friend, Donna Daugherty, who purchased a wild-caught African Grey parrot at a swap meet 14 years ago. She bought the bird because she felt sorry for it, and optimistically named it, "Gabby." Donna worked every day to teach Gabby to talk.

She would try different words and phrases, and use a lot of emphasis each time, but without any luck. Finally, on a bad day, she exasperatingly said, "Hello, stupid!" and Gabby repeated the phrase! Suddenly, Gabby had a whole little repertoire of the many things Donna had been trying to teach:

"Hello, Stupid! You big jerk! Hi, my name is Gabby. I'm a grey bird. Everybody knows that birds can't talk. Wheeeee, I can fly! Nobody loves me... Supercalifragilisticexpiali-oh sh—! My god, are you ugly!"

I was so amazed when Donna told me her bird could say all of these things, I went over to her house to hear it for myself, but the bird would not say a thing. Finally, I had Donna tape record the bird talking, so I could hear it, and so I could play it for customers that were curious how greys talk. That was 11 years ago, and I had to convince people that if they purchased an African Grey parrot, it would learn to talk. Nowadays, I don't have to prove anything to my customers; most of them walk in the door knowing that the African Grey has the best reputation for being a top-notch talker.

Tapes and Compact Discs

Many bird owners like to start their bird with speech lessons in the form of a tape or CD; this is fine as long as you limit the amount of time you play the tape for your bird. If you play a speech training tape over and over again, your bird will become bored with it, and learn to "tune it out" which will work against your good intentions. You will have greater success if you play a speech training tape twice a day for 30 minutes or less. The rest of the time you should supplement the bird's training lessons with a radio playing, or the television. Birds love to watch television, especially children's programs such as Sesame Street® and Nickelodeon®.

If you want to make your own speech training tape, you have two options: (1) Buy a long-playing tape and repeat several different words and/or phrases over and over again, or (2) buy an endless loop tape (like the kind used in an answering machine) and record one or two phrases. If you use the endless loop tape, you will need to turn off the tape player yourself, or put it on a timer, because otherwise it will just keep playing.

It is extremely important that you play your speech training tape while you are at home - don't pop in a tape or CD just before leaving the house. The reason for this is because you want your bird to associate talking and learning new phrases while you are around, not while you are away!

Sometimes the bird will learn to speak only when you are not home.

It is also important to vary the words and phrases you want to teach the bird, and that you choose new words, phrases, or tapes at least once a month. Your bird might not like the things you have selected, or it may need a break, and one or two months later it may decide to learn something new.

Repetition

Simple repetition is always a good teaching tool for speech training. For example, every morning, say (with enthusiasm) "Good morning!" to your grey. Each time you give it a snack, or treat, say something like, "Yum yum-that looks good! Want a bite?" And at bedtime, "Good night!" You will be surprised how quickly birds learn when there is a repetition to a phrase, and it is said with inflection. Another technique that really seems to stimulate speech is to get very close to the bird; practically face to face, and use a lot of emotion in your speech training.

The Informal Approach

If you purchase a bird that is known for outstanding talking ability, you can get away with the informal approach to speech training: doing nothing at all. Most greys pick up on their own, and learn to say the names of all of the family members, and may even call them by name. Greys love swear words, so you must be careful if you occasionally use colorful language, because you can bet your bird will instantly copy those exciting phrases!

Because our society is so busy working and supporting their families, it is hard for most people to take the time to have formal speech lessons for their birds. I think this is why African Greys are so well-liked, because they require little or no effort with speech training on our part, and they usually learn to say a lot of interesting things!

Out of the Beaks of Greys

Here is a list of noises from our survey birds that were learned:

Laughing
Crying
Barking
Meows
Imitate Cockatiels & Other Bird Noises

51

Wolf Whistle
Ticking Clock
Car Alarm
Coughs
Burps
Sneezes
Clears Throat
Blows Nose
Sound of a bomb falling, then exploding
Other miscellaneous obscene noises!

Here is a list of some of the more unusual spoken words and phrases from the survey birds:

Can you say hello?
Trick or Treat!
Merry Christmas
Ho! Ho! Ho!
Merry Turkey
That's really cool/that's cool
Peek-a-boo!
Ow! Ow! Ow!
Don't Poop on the Carpet!
I'm hungry! Go eat, eat, eat!
Could I have a Pretzel please?
Knock it off!
Be Quiet!
Will you quit that?!
Come Kiss
Mom loves you
I love you; I love you too!
What's your problem?
Want some scrambled eggs?
Want some water?
Want some scrambled water?
I have to go bye-bye
Bye-bye little girl
I love you
What?
How are you handsome?
Bye, bye, see ya later I have to go to work
Mama, let me out, come on, let me out!
Cool!
Right on!
Rock and Roll!
Breakfast! - It's Good for a Bird!
Go take a bath

I'm a plucked chicken
How about a cheeseburger?
Rrr, rrr, start the car!
Harr, harr, pirate bird!
I'm a pooper
Here kitty!
What's the matter?
Are you okay?
Help me, help!
Where's the gun-shoot it! Bang! Bang!
Tickle tickle!
Are you the pretty bird?
Bye-bye, Daddy has to go to work to make
   money to buy bird food!

My friends Steve and Cyndee Garvin raise African Greys and other birds and they kept one of the largest babies from a pair of Congos four years ago. They determined that the bird was a male and named him "Hercules". Hercules lives in a corner of their living room next to a large fish tank. He started talking around one year old, and now learns a new phrase in about two days. He may greet a visitor by saying, "Hi there!" or, "You look marvelous..." He also imitates every bird in Steve and Cyndee's nursery, including macaws, cockatoos, pionus, and poicephalus parrots. Interestingly, he will not imitate the baby greys. The house is shared by four dogs, and Hercules knows the difference between each dog's bark, and even if he cannot see the dog, he will call out its name, and tell it to be quiet!

Many greys love to have a sort of "run-on phrase" that they like to repeat; Hercules has one that he likes to say:

"Could ya, would ya, ain'tcha gonna? Aw, come on, ya said ya would... Now what's a matter? Won't your mama let you, huh?"

Regina Rahm owns a 3 year-old Congo grey which she named Cognac. Her philosophy towards owning and speech training a grey: "If you love your bird, he will love you back." At three years of age she estimates that he says approximately 250 words (many are phrases and sentences). She has a few question/answer responses that she and Cognac like to say together:

Regina: "What's your name?"
Cognac: "Poo poo bird!"
Regina: "That's your nickname"
Cognac: "My name is Cognac!"

Regina: "Cognac, Where's the kitty?"
Cognac: "Here, kitty, kitty, kitty...meow"
Regina: "Where is the doggie?"
Cognac: "Cognac speak! Woof! Woof! Woof!"

Regina: "What did you learn in school today?"
Cognac: "Alphabet! A, B, C, D"
Regina: "What else?"
Cognac: "1, 2, 3, 4, 5, 6"

Chapter 11

Trick Training

Because of our busy schedules and lack of free time, I have noticed less owners working with their birds and teaching them tricks. Trick training is teaching a bird one or more behaviors that can be performed on command. Almost every bird is capable of learning tricks and behaviors on cue; some are just more willing to perform than others. Because African Greys are so intelligent, they are the ideal students for trick training, because they can (if they want to!) learn a behavior very quickly.

The best way to start training your bird is to work with it when it is young. Greys don't like to be handled much, and if you work with them on lying on their back, playing dead, and other behaviors at an early age, they are more likely to tolerate you touching them all over.

I do not believe in withholding seed or food to reward a bird in training. I do believe that it is a good idea to try to offer the bird a small favorite treat, such as a pine nut, or small food item as a treat when they perform well for you. I also advocate a lot of praise: whenever your bird tries to do a behavior, or successfully completes the behavior, tell the bird, "Good bird! All right!" and reinforce your trick training behaviors with a lot of positive reinforcement.

One of the fun things to do with a tame parrot is to teach it to perform tricks and behaviors. Some birds love being the center of attention, and will perform for almost everyone, while others are more shy, and may not always want to be the star of the show (just like humans). It is important to already have a good relationship with your bird, and to be able to handle the bird without difficulty; a bird that is only semi-tame will not appreciate being rolled on its back, and it may hinder your efforts to gain its trust if you try to teach it a behavior it is not ready for yet.

Important Note: Limit training sessions to no more than 10 or 15 minutes once or twice a day; your bird will become bored or frustrated after longer periods of time. Also, if you continue to work on a behavior and your bird doesn't seem interested, move on to something else. You may work on several behaviors at the same time, just keep your lessons short, and work on the behaviors in the same order each time.

Trick #1: Get the Peanut

This is a classic bird show behavior. You need a T-stand, about two feet of thin cotton rope, some peanuts, and a small bucket (these can be found at craft stores, or you can make your own).

Tie the rope to the handle of the bucket, and then tie it to the T-stand. Put your bird on the T-stand and show it that you are putting a peanut into the bucket. Tell the bird to get the peanut, and see if it grabs the rope and starts to pull it up; if it doesn't, you can tie the rope up higher, and hang the bucket about 6 inches from the T-stand. At this point, your bird may lean down and just take the peanut out of the bucket-if he/she does, reward the bird with praise, and re-tie the rope a little longer, and put another peanut inside the bucket. Eventually, the bird will pull the rope all the way up by itself, and it makes a cute behavior.

Note: You may substitute another treat for the peanut if you wish.

Trick #2: Playing Dead

Young birds that have just weaned are the perfect age for this trick, and older birds can learn it too. It is important that your bird already feel comfortable on its back before you try to teach it this behavior. If the bird is not comfortable on its back, then you must first practice holding your bird, facing you, against your chest, and bend over slightly. Be sure one hand is under the bird's feet, and the other is on its back. When you practice bending over, start supporting the bird on its back on your hand. Keep bending over longer and longer periods of time, and let the bird feel comfortable resting in your hand. Then practice laying the bird in your hand without bending over. In a short time the bird should feel more comfortable on its back. Older birds may take longer to get accustomed to this, so be patient.

Place your bird on the floor or on a soft surface, and pretend to "shoot" it with your hand (in a pistol gesture). Say, "Bang! Dead bird..." then gently roll your bird onto its side and hold it there for a few seconds. Keep practicing the same way, and increasing the number of seconds you hold the bird on its side or back: work up to 20 seconds, then try it without holding the bird; if the bird lays still for a few seconds, praise it, then pick it up, and praise it again.

Note: Some people vary this trick slightly and hold the bird on their hand, then the bird will flip over backwards (while the owner holds its feet). If you think your bird would feel more comfortable doing this trick on your hand, go ahead and try it that way.

Trick #3: Birdie Headstand

This is not only a trick for greys, but it is also a great trick for small birds, such as lovebirds, poicephalus, and conures. The bird must first be able to lay comfortably on its back in your hand. Once the bird can do this you simply lay it on its back, on the palm of your hand, with its head closer to you, and its tail closer to your fingertips. Slowly bend upwards your four fingers, so your hand is no longer flat, but is in an L shape. Tell the bird you want it to stand on its head, and gently hold its tail while you lower your fingers back down. The bird will actually be balanced on its shoulders, but it will look like it is standing on its head. Hold this position for a second or two, and work up to five or ten seconds. Reward and praise the bird each time, and once the bird gets the idea, you will be able to position him instantly on your hand.

Trick #4: The Wave

Birds use their feet for many things other than perching, and many can be taught to wave. You need to put your bird on a perch or T-stand and lift up one of its feet (always use the same foot) and say, "Wave, Max, wave..." and then release the foot and praise the bird. It helps if you wave at your bird with your opposite hand at the same time, so later all you have to do is wave at your bird, and he will wave back.

Trick #5: Shake Hands

This trick is very easy to teach because birds like the attention they get. As often as you think of it, walk up to your bird and say, "Max, shake my hand" and pick up one of its feet (always the same one) with your index finger, and gently "shake" its foot, in an up and down motion. If you do this to your bird several times a day, he or she will pick it up in less than a week. Most birds will respond when someone else approaches them, puts out their index finger and asks to "shake their hand".

Other Tricks

Many of the survey respondents said that their greys liked to play "Peek-a-boo", lay on their back in their owner's hand, be held upside down and rocked, blow kisses, shake their head, wave goodbye, do an "Eagle" (full wings spread out), lift one wing, ring a bell on command, hang upside down, shake hands, and roll over.

Rick Morrow taught Dusty, his Congo African Grey, how to wave on command.

Diana Craven's Congo grey, Sabrina, will hang backward over the edge of her bed and say "tickle, tickle" to get her belly rubbed. Mary Josselson's Timneh, Alexandra (Allie for short), will catch a ball, and play hide and seek. Veradell Ballard's Congo, Willie, likes to dance to music with an audience; when they applaud he bows! Jill Arenson can hold up a glass of water and her Congo grey, Boris, will say, "some water!"

The important thing to remember when trick training your African Grey is to not expect too much; some birds are very animated and like to do these types of things, while other birds are quite happy being left alone. Some birds display funny, natural behaviors that can be made into a trick, so don't overlook your bird's behaviors and actions. You never know, you might have a star on your hands!

Many African Greys love to lay on their backs for their owners. Photo of Niaya by Diane Gallagher.

Chapter 12

Behavior Problems

African Greys are just like any other pet, and they require proper care, feeding, and upbringing; behavior problems usually arise from the owner's actions. You may feed, water, and clean your bird's cage diligently, but if you do not establish your bird's "place" in your household, and discipline it when it oversteps it's boundries, then you will experience behavior problems. In this chapter I will discuss in depth biting and screaming, because those are the two most common behavior problems. I have purposely devoted an entire chapter to feather picking, because I feel that it is a symptom of captivity, rather than a behavior problem. (Some owners do perpetuate the feather picking and make it a behavior problem, but more will be said about that in Chapter 13.)

Important Note: I feel that owners of large parrots should train them to sit on their hand or arm, but not the shoulder. The reason for this is because birds that sit on their owner's shoulders tend to feel equal or superior to their owner, and therefore they tend to misbehave more. Because they are in an awkward place to retrieve, it makes it difficult to manage a bird when it is on your shoulder, and some bird owners have been bitten on the face due to this. This applies to all large hookbilled birds!

Biting

Most hand-fed African Grey parrots do not learn that they have the capability to bite someone and get a reaction until they are about 6-9 months old. It is very important that if you purchase a baby African Grey that you do not let it "teethe" or nibble on your fingers and hands, similar to owning a new puppy. If you do, it is more reason for your bird to think it is allowed to do this to you later, and it will be a much harder nibble! Rather than say, "NO! Don't Bite!" to a young bird, it is better to distract and engage the bird in some other activity, without scolding it. For example, let's say your baby grey starts nibbling on your fingernails, or fingers; pick up a millet spray, and move your fingers away from the bird and immediately offer the millet for the bird to chew on, while you say, "Here, baby, go ahead and chew on this..." If you always repeat this technique, you will subconsciously train the bird that your fingers and hands are not for its beak to gnaw on.

Birds that are already past the baby stage are delighted that they have found an effective way to get their owners attention. It is more painful now if you are bitten, but what you do, and how you follow through will impact your relationship with the bird for a long time. If you yell loudly, and put the bird down, and act afraid around the bird everytime you try to handle it, you are going to be mincemeat! Greys love to intimidate humans, and it is their way of having the last say-so. If your grey is in the adolescent stages of its life, then you may be able to have a slight confrontation with it to establish the "pecking order" in your house.

As soon as your bird starts to pinch or bite you, immediately drop your hand so the bird must lose its balance. Usually it will release its bite, but keep watching the bird, because some will immediately try again. The reason they try again is to see if you are going to follow through (just like a child) or, if you will let them get their way. Some birds like to instigate trouble because it is a game to them.

Important Note: One deterrent for biting is to try putting soap or Bitter Apple® on your hands; once your bird tastes something bad, it may stop biting.

Another technique that is a little tricky, but works quite well is to hold your grey's upper and lower mandible together for a few seconds, immediately after it has tried to bite you. Use your thumb on top of the upper mandible, and your forefinger underneath the lower mandible; while you say a firm, "No!" You must use caution when going for the bird this way, because if you miss, you will be bitten even worse. Birds don't like to be held against their will, especially when someone else is in control. Your goal is to hopefully be able to just say "No!" and the bird will release its beak.

Older greys that are set in their ways are very difficult to break from biting. These birds are wise beyond their years, and they can deliver a very nasty bite. My best advice to owners of greys like this is to be very cautious and enjoy the bird for its talking and personality talents. Don't push the bird, especially on someone you don't know who might be hurt unsuspectingly. It is also important to avoid placing birds on your shoulder that are unpredictable.

Important Note: Some birds bite out of fear, versus birds that bite intentionally. It is important that you recognize the difference, and if your bird is biting out of fear, that you do not reprimand, or punish the bird, because it is only reacting instinctively, and it is truly fearful that it's life is at stake. Some of the reasons birds bite out of fear are: catching a bird for grooming, biting during grooming, biting when a new toy is introduced too quickly, biting a person that the bird is not used to, biting its owner because he or she looks different, (or is wearing brightly colored clothes), biting its owner because there is a new pet quickly approaching the bird and it is afraid. Reasons birds bite out of spite are: going back inside their cage when they are not "ready", biting one owner because someone is coming near that they do not like, biting the owner when they put their hand inside the cage, and deliberately running over to someone to bite them.

Screaming

Fortunately, most African Greys have pleasant, resonant jungle noises that are loud, but not offensive. However, if you have more than one bird in the household and the other birds have an annoying scream, your grey will inevitably learn to copy the noises that bother you the most. I always like to warn people of this fact when they purchase a grey, because if they decide to buy another bird later on, they may think carefully about what kind of bird to buy.

We once sold a grey to a client that also owned a macaw. The grey learned to mimic the macaw so well, that the owner finally sold the grey because she couldn't stand it. This particular grey never really made any macaw noises in our store, nor did it seem to have any problems in its second home. I believe that birds do things for a reason, and it is possible that this bird did not feel comfortable in the same home with the macaw.

If your grey has learned an annoying yell, or sound, the worst thing you can do is make a big deal out of it. If you whisper or say some alternate phrase to the bird, it may lose interest and say something else to get your attention. If that doesn't work, you may try one of the following methods:

(1) "Time Out" This technique is similar to reprimanding a small child. If the bird will not refrain from screaming, take it to the nearest bathroom for time out. Make sure the lid to the toilet is securely fastened, and that there is no water in the sink or bathtub. Place the bird inside the bathtub, and close the shower doors. If you have a shower curtain, remove the magnets out of the corners, and place the curtain on the outside of the bathtub. If there are windows or blinds in the bathroom, close them, and turn out the lights before you leave.

You may leave your bird inside the bathroom for 5 to 10 minutes, but no longer than that. When you go to retrieve your bird, be sure to tell it that you want it to be a good bird, or you will have to return it for another time out. Your bird may test you to see if you are going to follow through, but usually once or twice is sufficient for most birds.

(2) Squirt Bottle - Many people feel the squirt bottle is cruel, however I raised my first two birds with the squirt bottle and I feel that if used correctly, it can be a useful (and not really needed) training tool. First of all, you never squirt the bird in the face, only from the neck down. Secondly, if you are going to mist your birds with a squirt bottle, you better make sure that your bathing squirt bottle looks completely different from your training squirt bottle. The best thing to do is to purchase a colored toy squirt gun, and use that as your training tool. This will always squirt in the "stream" mode, whereas a spray bottle can be adjusted to the "mist" mode, which feels more natural and pleasant to the bird.

When do you use the squirt gun for behavior modification? When the bird starts an undesirable behavior. For example, if your bird is learning how to climb down off of its cage and wander, as soon as the bird is descending, say, "Shadow, get back on your cage!" and if the bird does not, use your squirt gun to squirt the bird in the chest area. If the bird returns to the cage top, reward it with praise, and tell it it is a good bird. If you keep the squirt gun within visual range of the bird, sometimes all you have to do is say, "I'm going to get the squirt gun..." and the bird will stop the behavior you are trying to prevent.

Some birds are undaunted by the squirt gun and will just give you a nasty look!

Important Note: Some bird behaviorists do not agree with time out or using squirt bottles or squirt guns. I believe that it is important that these training techniques are used in moderation, and that a bird should never be punished for more than five or ten minutes in time out, and never be squirted in a vengeful manner. I have always used these techniques in a considerate, humane manner, and they have been helpful for me and my birds.

Throwing Things

African Greys love to learn the secrets of tossing their food and sometimes water bowls. Some greys will throw food on the floor, especially after you are finished vacuuming!

These are behaviors that occur because (1) They get a big reaction and (2) They are bored and looking for things to do. The best thing to do is to find locking bowl holders and hooded crocks for the seed. Locking bowl holders may feature a screw-lock on the outside of the cage, fastening the bowl securely to the cage, or the ring that holds the bowl may have a screw that you adjust over the edge of the crock so the bird cannot lift and throw the bowl down. Hooded crocks are very helpful to prevent birds from defecating in their food or water, and because of their design deter birds from throwing their seeds. Some birds may be afraid of the hooded crocks at first, so be sure to check that your bird is eating. Many greys love to talk into the hooded crocks to hear their own "echo".

Once you have secured your grey's feed bowls, you may wish to find some interesting hand-held toys for your grey to throw around!

Chapter 13

Feather Picking

You may have purchased this book strictly for this one chapter; feather picking is becoming a universal problem for all birds in captivity. There are still many unknown factors, and few successful methods, to treat feather picking. African Grey parrots have a higher chance for becoming feather pickers probably due to their increased intelligence.

Comparing Congos, Ghanas and Timnehs, I have observed less Timnehs feather picking than Congos or Ghanas. This could be for two reasons: (1) There are less Timnehs available and; (2) it is my opinion Timnehs seem to handle stress slightly better than the Congos and Ghanas. Of the Congos and Ghanas that I have seen pick their feathers, the ones most affected are mostly female and usually "spoiled" in their home atmosphere. These are not neglected birds, usually quite the opposite. Are we killing our birds with kindness? It's possible.

I will start with what to do the FIRST time if your African Grey picks its feathers, and then categorize the typical reasons for feather picking into four categories: (1) Stress in the Environment, (2) Boredom & Extra Attention, (3) Sexual Maturity, and (5) Physical Deficiency.

**What to do if your Grey picks its feathers
for the very FIRST time:**

First of all, you do not want to call attention to the bird, or walk up to the bird and say, "Shadow, What have you done??" The tone of your voice, and your body language communicate to your bird that you are unhappy, and your bird will get a sense of uneasiness from this type of confrontation. Also, do NOT say to your grey, "Don't pick your feathers!" because the bird will later associate the picking with the verbal attention.

If your bird just started picking its feathers, chances are there is someone, or something new in your house that is bothering the bird. This could be a visiting relative, or a new painting on the wall. It could be new furniture, or a new plant. It could also be another animal in the house.

Debbie Schneider has a 14 month old Congo named Casey and a cat in her home. When the cat started sleeping on the bottom shelf of her cage, Casey started picking the top feathers around the front of her neck. When Debbie stopped the cat from sleeping on the bird's cage, Casey stopped plucking. This does not mean that all greys are afraid of cats, because they are not, but it is simply an example of how a grey can become uncomfortable in its own home.

Try to find the source of your grey's stress, and if it is a new piece of furniture, put it on the opposite side of the room and tell the bird that it's okay to be afraid of something new, and slowly move the furniture closer to its final destination. Hold your grey and walk by the object it is afraid of and reassure the bird.

Usually removing the object that is scaring your bird will deter the bird from continuing to feather pick as long as you catch it in the early stages. Most people react so strongly when their birds first start to pick their feathers that they miss the reason the bird is picking in the first place, and this only perpetuates the problem.

Other Instances of Feather Picking:

Stress in the Environment

Our pet birds are like our children, and even though they don't share responsibilities managing the household, they absorb the daily joys and stresses that ripple through all the members of the family. As I have mentioned before, birds really have few means of relieving tension, and therefore, many begin to pick their feathers as a release.

Boredom

African Greys are so smart, they love to watch people, play with toys, and play games with family members or other pets in the household. If there is no intellectual stimulus in the home, the bird may become bored and resort to chewing its feathers to occupy itself. Taking the bird out of its cage, giving it a play tree, and taking it out of the house are all healthy stimuli (even though many birds do not like it, they are distracted and the change is good).

Sexual Maturity

When Timnehs are approximately two years old, and Congos and Ghanas are between three and four years of age, they are nudging sexual maturity. Some birds experience hormone surges that cause behavior changes, mood swings, and possible feather picking. It is important to circle the days on a calendar every time your grey picks its feathers, because if it is hormonal, you will see a rise and fall in the feather picking. This type of feather picking is the easiest to control, because it usually subsides on its own, and if the bird is given lots of chew toys, or paper, it may not chew on its own feathers as much.

Physical Deficiency/Chemical Imbalance

It is my belief that many of the pet birds that feather pick and self-mutilate today are doing so because it is a symptom of their being a pet bird and lack of exercise. Birds in the wild fly from place to place every day, unless there is bad weather, and then they are exposed to the ultraviolet rays of the sun, and fresh air and change in environment.

I have no way of testing my theory, but I believe that just like when humans exercise and create chemical reactions within their bodies, birds do the same. Maybe there is some sort of enzyme that is lacking in a pet bird's body that creates a symptom of feather picking, or self-mutilation. Maybe research in the future can try to address this area and we can synthetically produce a supplement that can "fool" the bird's brain and prevent the picking problems.

Solutions to Feather Picking

There are no permanent solutions to feather picking, however, there are many steps you can take to control feather picking, and hopefully keep it down to a minimum. We should look in the future for more information regarding more holistic approaches, and possibly acupuncture and/or acupressure for birds.

Bathing, Feather Sprays, Humidity

Never use a bird bath spray on your African Grey; almost all are made with Purcellin, a synthetic oil which is okay to use on a South American bird, because it has an oil gland, but African Greys and Cockatoos have a powder gland and a liberal dusting of powder on their feathers, and this type of bath spray is bad for the bird's feathers.

Misting a bird with plain water is recommended on a daily basis for all African Greys. Most of the larger Greys originate from a wet region that receives a large amount of rainfall, so it is important to take your bird into the shower for the steam, or to bathe it regularly, even if it is missing a lot of feathers. It really does help. Bird owners in very dry climates may wish to purchase a room humidifier for their greys.

Bitter extract sprays rarely seem to work on an African Grey. I have experienced many customer's frustration when they purchased this type of spray and found that the bird only picked more furiously after being sprayed with a bitter-tasting spray. I think these birds are too smart for this, unfortunately.

Vitamins & Diet

It never hurts to try using a new vitamin and mineral supplement with your African Grey; this can sometimes work quite well. We have noticed about a 40% success rate in controlling (notice I didn't say curing) feather picking by using a product made by Vitakraft called ProFeda®. It is a syrup consisting of calcium, phosphorus, and riboflavin, and it is added to the drinking water. It is not good for birds that are overweight, because it has dextrose in it. The birds don't seem to mind it, and it can be used instead of a calcium supplement.

Calcium is important, and it may be provided in the form of cuttlebone, or calcium powder. The most popular brand of calcium is Fort Dodge's D-Ca-Fos®, which is calcium with vitamin D_3 added. Most aviculturists don't realize, however, that too much vitamin D_3 can be toxic, so it is important that you get the proper dose for your bird. We simply serve a lot of cuttlebone (wedged in the bars of the cage) and sprinkle D-Ca-Fos® three times a week on the fruit and vegetable bowl.

There is a liquid calcium supplement, NeoCalglucon®, which can be added to the water instead of powder on the fruit. Usual dosage is one teaspoon in a 12-ounce crock of water, or 3 cc's per 4 ounces of water.

Many bird breeders are experimenting with Spirulina and Wheat Grass Powder to improve their birds plumage. I have not seen many greys on this type of supplementation, but it may also be an option to try.

Diet changes can affect an African Grey's feathers also. Many Greys seem to benefit from some of the pelleted diets, and most grey owners still let their birds have a spoonful of seeds in addition to their pellets, fruits and vegetables, and any table food. It is possible that there could be something important lacking in their diet that is causing the feather picking.

Notching the Beak

Many years ago a customer described to us a technique that his veterinarian used to curb feather plucking. This technique involves dremeling a notch in the lower mandible so when the bird attempts to pull out a feather it simply slips through the beak. (The bird no longer has the same grip as before.) The beak grows very quickly, so the notch only lasts about 3 weeks. Some birds may respond after one or two times of notching the beak, and I recommend that the owner leave the bird alone, if it is improved.

We have used this technique on many greys (Congos, Ghanas and Timnehs) with much success. If done correctly, it is not painful to the bird, and there is no bleeding. The only problem we have encountered is that after a few times of notching a bird's lower mandible, some of the greys learned to clamp their jaws shut so we were unable to open the beak to notch it!

Here is how to notch the beak: (The equipment I use is a Dremel® Mini-Mite with a #952-cone-shaped stone tip.)

First, put the upper mandible inside the lower mandible.

Normal Beak *Beak After Notching*

Next, dremel a 1/8-3/16" groove in the center of the lower mandible. Be sure to lightly file the corners of the beak so they are not sharp.

A Case History

I have been following an individual Congo African grey's history with feather plucking. "Batman" is a $3^1/2$ year old grey owned by Dean and Rebecca Cockerham who purchased the bird as a domestic baby. The first five months they had Batman, they lived with roommates with children, and there were people around twenty-four hours a day. Then they moved to a home with just the three of them. Dean and Rebecca both work, so they are gone 9-10 hours a day. As you can imagine, this was probably what triggered Batman to pick her feathers, and she did a very complete job of it.

There are several factors that I believe enhanced the intensity of Batman's plucking: (1) The sudden change in her environment; birds feel that everyone in their home is part of their "flock" and when Dean and Rebecca moved, Batman felt abandoned in a way; (2) Batman is a female Congo African Grey-for some reason female greys tend to pluck their feathers more than male birds; it could be because they long for the men in the household, and in many households, men work longer hours and are not available to pets as much as women.

I have seen several other cases where greys picked this severely, but fortunately, most greys that feather pick do so in smaller areas, or less frequently. The problem that occurs with greys that feather pick severely is that even if the bird stopped picking its feathers, there are so many severely damaged and split feather remnants all over the bird's body, especially on the wings and tail, that it is impossible for the bird to remove these damaged feathers so new ones can grow in. Some of these damaged remants will molt out, but for some reason, I notice that they tend to just remain there, unable to serve any purpose. I try to pluck just a few of these mangled remains of a feather each time I groom a feather plucker, in hopes that the bird will leave the new feather alone. This is a very stressful procedure for the bird, and I use small needlenose pliers to remove a damaged, broken-off feather. You should only pull two to four feathers in one sitting, and if you do not pull the feather out correctly, you can damage the feather shaft. You must use extra caution with the wings, because if you do not pull the feather in the same direction it grows, and you do not hold the wing correctly, you can break their wing.

Photo of Batman before notching the lower mandible.

Photo of Batman several months later after notching the beak every 30 days.

We notched Batman's beak every three weeks for several months, and noticed improvement with her feathers. (Rebecca also misted Batman with water daily.) However, as soon as the beak would grow back, she would promptly destroy whatever progress had been made. Then the day came when she learned how to clamp her upper and lower mandible shut so I could not open her beak, much less notch it anymore. Finally, I "made a deal" with Batman after several months with struggling to notch her beak. I looked the bird in the eye, and promised the bird that I would not notch her beak anymore if she would leave her feathers alone. The next time I saw the bird her feathers were improved! It may be coincidence, but her owners and I have decided to try whatever seems to work!

Her current status: Batman continues to have feather problems, but many are old, damaged, split feathers that need to be molted, or pulled. I see her every three to four weeks for maintenance, and Rebecca and Dean have decided that if she leaves her wing feathers alone (which she has done since our verbal "agreement") they are going to leave her fully-flighted. They are willing to take the proper safety precautions for her in their home if it is the key to helping her "kick the habit".

The most amazing thing about this case history is the fact that Batman is one of the nicest greys I have met. Everytime she comes in for her "beauty treatments" she is always good natured and forgiving. I always say hello to her before I get started, tell her what I am going to do, and apologize profusely when I am done. I can tell that this bird is content, and VERY patient. An even more remarkable discovery, however, is the fact that on their survey, I ask the question, "Are you happy with your grey, and if you had it to do all over again, would you purchase a grey?" And Dean and Rebecca would. I think that says something about the type of devotion grey owners possess.

I remember a Congo grey in the past whose owner told me when I purchased it,"Whatever you do, do not clip his wings, or he will start picking his feathers!" When I bought the bird, he was in beautiful feather, and he lived on the side of her home in an outdoor aviary. The bird had some filtered sunlight, but nothing too intense. The bird had a mate and they both had run of the aviary, which they seemed to enjoy. His previous owner also gave him a new telephone book every few months to rip up.

I still believe that there is some connection between feather picking and the lack of fresh air, natural sunlight, and the ability to fly.

Medications

Many veterinarians are experimenting with human anti-depressant drugs to treat African Greys with obsessive compulsive feather picking behaviors. I don't feel that drugs are a permanent solution, so I question their benefits to birds. Valium is also commonly prescribed, however, just like with humans, narcotic drugs are addictive and birds that are treated with these medications must be slowly weaned off of them also.

Collars

Occasionally a veterinarian will recommend an Elizabethan Collar for a bird with a severe picking or self-mutilation problem. Collars should be reserved for extreme cases only, because greys tend to really stress out when they get the collar put on. Some collars are handmade out of X-ray film, while others are thick plastic with snaps. There is a newer collar available that resembles a neck brace, and it is made out of hard plastic. This collar fastens with metal or plastic screws, and these features make it more "bird-proof".

Acupuncture

I was fortunate to recently learn about acupuncture for birds from Michal Partington, D.V.M. Dr. Partington took his certification course in acupuncture from the International Veterinary Acupuncture Society in 1987-1988. At that time the curriculum did not include detailed information on psittacine birds, and Dr. Partington began the task of collecting Chinese charts on chickens and ducks. He then correlated the underlying anatomy (the arteries, veins and nerves) similar to man, and formulated acupuncture points for psittacines. In 1990, he started teaching acupuncture to veterinarians, and he is currently seeing clients that desire his expertise in this field of work.

This is how acupuncture works:

(1) The veterinarian must have an experienced technician that can expertly hold the bird and not induce stress to the bird;

(2) Sterile, disposable human acupuncture needles (of the smallest sizes) are used by the veterinarian.

(3) Approximately 12 needles, 6 on each side, are inserted in the acupuncture points on the bird. Birds have two main areas for acupuncture points: between the elbow and the tip of the wing, and between the knee and the toes. The needles are inserted just under the skin, or into the muscle. Most are shallow insertions. The veterinarian may do both sides at the same time, or one side at a time.

(4) The needles are then removed, and the total procedure takes approximately 15-20 minutes.

(5) After the treatment the bird feels relaxed, and has experienced similar to what humans call a "Runner's high," which is an endorphin release.

Dr. Partington stresses that it is important to cross check the bird's medical history before attempting acupuncture to rule out physical illness. The majority of his patients are what he calls psychogenic feather pickers - their problem is not due to a physical ailment, but a result of emotional stress.

A normal treatment for most birds consists of two treatments to start, one week apart. After that, Dr. Partington usually will not need to give additional treatments for anywhere from six months to one year. There are exceptions, however, and Dr. Partington also emphasizes that it is critical for the bird owner to learn to interpret what is causing their bird's stress, and to eliminate or reduce the factors that are to blame. Otherwise additional treatments will be necessary. You must treat the problem in addition to the symptom!

I am intrigued and optimistic that acupuncture may be able to help many birds (and their owners) in need of help with feather picking.

For a list of veterinarians that may have interest in acupuncture, see the address for the International Veterinarian Acupuncture Society in the back of the book to locate a veterinarian in your area.

Chapter 14

Socializing a New Baby Grey

When you take home a baby African Grey that is either still hand-feeding once or twice a day, or is already weaned, you may immediately start to play with and socialize your bird. Many of the older training books recommended waiting a few days before handling your bird to let it get comfortable, but that applied to wild-caught birds that were extremely frightened, and benefited from any respite in handling they were allowed. Domestic, hand-fed birds adapt to new environments and people with much more ease than their wild relatives.

Many people are so thrilled to purchase their first African Grey that they do not realize how important it is to establish some guidelines regarding who handles the bird, for how long, and how to begin training the family to behave with the bird.

Baby African Greys should be introduced to their cage as early as possible; preferably around 8 or 9 weeks of age. Even if they play and sleep in a dishtub, you can put the tub inside the cage when you are not home, and the bird will accept it's new cage much easier. Line the dishtub with newspaper and a non-toxic bedding material - a good one is Carefresh®. You may wish to line the trays in the cage the same way; babies that are hand-feeding have more runny stools, and you will save the metal on your trays if you first line the tray with paper. In a baby bird's dishtub do not use corn cob litter, cedar shavings or shavings treated with chlorophyll, because these can be harmful if they are eaten by the baby. If you are not using a dishtub, and there is a grill inside of the cage, you can use what ever type of bedding you prefer, because the bird will not be able to eat it. If you wait until the bird is almost weaned to introduce it to a cage, it may not like the cage you have selected for it, and it will take the bird longer to get adjusted.

It is also important to trim your baby African Grey's wings and file the sharp edges off the nails. Babies should have what I call a "Baby Clip" around 7 or 8 weeks of age. Because their feathers are still growing, this clip is very temporary, and only slightly limits their mobility. Do not take a baby African Grey outside unless it is in a carrier because it may be able to fly better than you think.

The "Baby Clip" consists of clipping the first 4 or 5 primary flight feathers, right below the covert feathers. See below:

A baby grey should have 4 or 5 primary flight feathers clipped.

Filing a baby African Grey's toenails is easy, and should be done by the owner once a week so the bird becomes used to this type of handling. Simply sit the bird down on a towel on your lap and use a professional emery board, medium coarseness, to file the sharp tips. Be sure to hold the toe and the toenail, because if you bend the toenail too hard, you may break the toe. File the nail in one direction, rather than back and forth, for the same reason. If you are experienced using a dremel, you may file the tips of the toenails rather quickly.

Baby birds are a lot like exercise equipment: at first a new exercise bike is used daily with great passion; as time goes by, the bike gets used less and less; eventually the bike may end up in the garage to collect dust! Unfortunately, many birds are purchased under the same conditions: the new owner brings home the bird and lavishes it with toys, fruits and vegetables, and a beautiful cage. At first, everyone in the home is anxious to handle the bird, and the bird receives a lot of attention. The owner makes sure he or she leaves the television or radio on for the bird, bathes the bird regularly, and takes it out for a walk once in a while, or a ride in the car. After awhile, however, the owner may be less interested in the bird, or tired of its mess on the bottom of the cage. Family members may lose interest in the bird, and the bird may eventually end up in the garage. This scenario has happened many times. As a bird store owner, it is my responsibility to prepare any potential parrot owner for the physical and emotional needs of a pet bird. As a bird owner, it is your responsibility to commit yourself to the care and well being of your new pet bird.

Here are nine basic rules to follow to help you socialize and behave properly around your new African Grey:

Rule #1: If you bring a new grey home, don't spend lots of extra time with it so that it will bond with you-it's going to bond with you anyway. Incorporate the bird into your daily routine, with at least 15 minutes of attention in the morning before you leave for work (this can even be letting the bird sit on the shower rod while you shower and get ready for work), at least 1-2 hours in the evening when you get home from work. (Always try to let the bird out of its cage as soon as you get home if it will play on its cage. Later you can sit and cuddle with it after you change your clothes, check for phone messages, etc.)

Rule #2: I recommend that you do not allow your African Grey to sit on your shoulder all of the time. Most bird behavior specialists also advise their clients to keep their bird on their hand or their arm. The shoulder is a very comfortable place for a bird - but it also makes the bird feel superior to its owner, and it is more likely to misbehave if you let it become a "shoulder bird." If you occasionally allow your bird on the shoulder to free both hands, that's different; you are controlling the bird, the bird is not controlling you.

Rule #3: Never let the bird (especially babies) lick and nibble or bite your fingers. Many bird stores feature mostly hand-fed babies that are still learning how to crack seeds and eat solid foods. When these birds see your fingers they think you are going to feed them. By allowing them to bite your fingers, you are teaching them that it's okay to bite hands. Later, when the bird is older, it will still be biting, only it will have its full beak pressure, and it will hurt! By this time it is difficult (but not impossible) to reverse this habit. It is best to give the baby bird small toys to chew instead of fingers; baby toys, leather strips and rubber dog bones are excellent placebos for fingers. It is not necessary to scold a baby that starts chewing your fingers; simply distract the bird with a suitable toy. When the bird is older (5 months or older) you may tell the bird, "No!" and quickly substitute a small chew toy instead of your hand. You need to be careful not to constantly scold the bird, or the word "no" won't mean anything.

Rule #4: Always use the "Step-Up" command when you want the bird to get on your hand. Very young birds sometimes don't even know how to get up on the hand or arm, so it is necessary to use two hands to pick the bird up; you may still tell the baby to "step up."

The reason why you tell the bird to step up is so that it will automatically respond when its owner wants to pick it up. You may also wish to use the "Down" command when you want to put the bird back on its cage; I just like to say to my bird, "Go Back."

Rule #5: Try to socialize your bird while it is young. Take your bird to family gatherings and invite friends to handle your bird when they come over to your home. (Always make sure people wash their hands with soap and water before handling your baby when it is young, because it is more susceptible to illness.) For some birds, this early socializing may make a difference in how they respond to other people; some birds bond tightly to their immediate owner or family, because as far as the bird is concerned, it has no need to accept any other "members" into its flock.

Rule #6: Don't overspoil your grey. Carrying your bird room to room, never leaving the bird in its cage to play, always taking the bird wherever you go, and always holding your bird when you are home can lead to serious behavior problems due to overspoiling your bird. It is important for you to sometimes be able to kick back on the couch without your bird, or sometimes put your bird in its cage to play while you are cleaning. It is also good to take the bird out for a ride, or to work with you, as long as it doesn't become something you have to do.

Rule #7: Don't reinforce bad behavior: If your bird likes to bite your spouse, do not pat it on the head and say, "Sammy! Don't bite Daddy-Come on and be a good boy and do what your Mommy says..." By patting the bird on the head and talking to it soothingly you are teaching the bird how to get more attention from an undesirable behavior. If your bird tries to bite your spouse when you hand it to him or her, tell the bird, "No bite!" and put the bird on the floor and walk out of the room. Now your spouse must "rescue" the bird, and the bird should be more passive, since it is on the floor.

Rule #8: NEVER hit your bird. It is possible to render the bird unconscious if you hit it hard enough. Even thumping a bird on the beak with your finger is wrong; it can also result in a bruise on your bird's beak. If your bird does something terrible, first try to think WHY your bird did what it did: Was he bored: Is he/she lonely and wants to mate? Birds do things usually for a reason, if you need help with your bird, don't hesitate to call someone experienced in bird behavior.

DO NOT punish your bird for days at a time—birds are like small children and quickly forget what they have done; most of the time the reason they bite or do something bad is because they are very excited and "caught up in the moment". Birds do not understand long term punishment, and it is cruel to do so.

Rule #9: Don't expect too much from your grey. African Greys are very beautiful, curious and intelligent creatures. They can be loyal, loving, spiteful, pesty, and a lot of work. They are also great company. Some birds will love learning new tricks. Others will enjoy nipping everyone that comes over to your home. A few will carry on a conversation with you. Don't expect your bird to learn a word or behavior just because you want it to. Read training manuals and talk to people that are experienced with birds, especially African Greys. Some birds have wonderful personalities, but their owners only see their shortcomings instead of their merits.

Baby African Greys are cute and cuddly, but don't overspoil a new bird!

Chapter 15

Buying a Used Grey

It is not very often that you will find a family selling its pet African Grey, nor will you see many older (meaning 1 year or older) greys for sale in a pet or bird store. This is probably due to the fact that these birds seem to integrate themselves into the household, and people don't want to let them go. Does this mean that all of the greys for sale are mean and nasty? No. Many of them are really nice birds with excellent vocabularies. How can you tell if an older bird is nice, and what steps should you take before purchasing a "used" grey?

First of all, if the bird is in a pet shop or bird store, the best thing to do is to ask the manager or owner what the bird's history is. Did the owners sell it because they didn't have time for it (the most common reason, but not always the "real" reason), or did the owner need to be relocated, or was there a death in the family? It is helpful to have an idea what the bird's background has been, if it was originally hand-raised, and if it prefers men or women. If it prefers one sex, and it does not like you, chances are it will not bond to you even in your home. Don't let anyone tell you otherwise, except the bird: if the bird likes you while it is in the store, chances are it will bond to you.

Second, ask the store if they are willing to give you compensation if the bird is not happy in one month's time. One month is really a short amount of time to judge how a bird is going to work out, but usually you will have an idea how things are going, and if the bird is not happy, see if the store will give you credit towards another bird.

Third, if you don't like the bird's name, don't change it right away, unless you think it is derogatory, or the bird doesn't seem to care. Birds get used to their name, and I feel it is best to keep their original name, especially if they say their name often.

What if the bird is for sale from a private party? Most private party want ads in the paper are sold "as is". Occasionally, you will find a family that is not desperate for money, and just wants to find their bird a good home, and they will offer to take the bird back (and refund your money) if the bird does not work out. Most times, however, this is not the case.

You can get a fairly good deal sometimes with a bird and a cage, but make sure you know what the going rate is on the bird and cage you are buying; what sounds like a good deal might be just as expensive as buying everything new at your local bird store, which may offer more services.

Most "used" birds are in need of grooming, and bathing. Before you leave, be sure and ask if there is any recent paperwork on the bird from their veterinarian. If there is, take this paperwork with you when you have the bird checked out so he or she can compare test results.

If you are buying the grey from a friend, the best thing to do is to visit the bird in your friend's home, and it doesn't hurt if you take it "presents" like a favorite treat, nut, or a small hand-held toy. If the bird likes you and looks forward to your visits, you should have the bird's owner tell the bird that you are going to give the bird a new home, and that it is a very lucky bird. Then you should also tell the bird you are excited to be its new owner, and you are going to take it home soon. The bird may not understand a word of what you are saying, however, the tone of your voice, and your good intentions are communicated to the bird. (Be sure the original owner can handle saying "good-bye"-a very dramatic, stressful good-bye scene is not recommended; in that case you should pick up the bird when the owner is not home!)

There are two main problems when it comes to buying a used grey: (1) Sometimes they like to bite, and they will bite often, so you need to be unafraid of the bird, and able to avoid bites and re-train the bird; (2) You inherit the bird's vocabulary, good and bad. A bird with a foul mouth is actually worth less than one that doesn't talk much. Be sure and ask if the bird says any swear words, and approximately how many.

My friend Diana Craven purchased one of her three greys from a couple that was divorcing, and for the longest time, the bird would repeat arguments it had heard in its first home!

I have seen many very nice older African Greys for sale that have turned out to be wonderful pets; don't discount the fact that they are "used" because they just might be the companion you are looking for.

Chapter 16

Breeding African Greys

African Grey Parrots are one of the easiest birds to breed, especially the Congos and the Ghanas. The Timnehs are a little more difficult, but definitely not impossible. The nice thing about breeding African Greys is the fact that even though they make a lot of jungle-type noises, they are fairly quiet, and most neighbors find their whistles and chirps very pleasant. This allows anyone in a mild climate to put their birds outside, which is recommended whenever possible.

There seem to be two keys to success when it comes to breeding African Greys: (1) Privacy and (2) Cage Size. If you own a healthy, mature pair of African Greys, and they are set up in a quiet, or semi-secluded area, in a not-too-large cage, they are most likely to breed within one or two years. I will review the guidelines for setting up greys; for more in depth information, you may wish to review my book, *Breeding Exotic Birds - A Beginner's Guide.*

Choosing Healthy Breeders

It is always desirable to choose a bird that looks healthy, and is a good weight, and has bright, clear eyes and clean nostrils. One nostril larger than the other may indicate an old injury or an old or recurring sinus infection. Check the inside of the mouth for any lesions (which could indicate a vitamin deficiency), and check the vent to make sure that it is clean. The beak should not be overgrown, and the beak and the feathers should appear dusty. Little lines or "cracks" on the beak is usually normal, and are enhanced by the dust from the feathers. If you think the bird's beak or nails needs filing or grooming, now is the time to do it. After the birds are set up for breeding, it will be a major event to try to get them to come out of their nest boxes.

Once you have purchased a single bird or breeder pair, it is a good idea to have your avian veterinarian perform a brief physical exam and recommend any testing. (See Chapter 3-Going to the Vet.) It is important to quarantine any new purchases before introducing them into your collection. Most breeders have rooms, or sections, that are designated for proven, established breeder pairs, and those areas are "closed" to subsequent pairs that may be purchased.

When you feed your entire collection of birds, you always feed the most valuable bird room first, then the next, and so on, until you get to the most recently set up breeding room, or area, so in the event your birds contract a bacteria or virus, it may not affect your entire collection. Be sure that you do not walk back and forth over the same hallway, or use the same cart in all different rooms, because then you are defeating your purpose of controlling disease. If you do have a common hallway, then place a foot bath (a dishtub with disinfectant in the bottom that you dip the bottom of your shoes into) at the entrance of each room. Be sure each room has its own feed bin, broom, dustpan, service cart, etc. That way you are not tracking anything from one room to the other.

Most breeders will isolate new pairs of birds while they are waiting for their lab results back from the veterinarian; some will riskily take the birds home and place them immediately into their breeding room. The choice will be yours each time you purchase a pair of birds. I can honestly say that there have been several occasions where I knew the full history of the birds being sold to me, and I felt comfortable taking them home and placing them in our #3 room-that's the room with the most recent purchases. Number 1 and number 2 rooms are closed, and therefore I am not exposing those birds to the new birds.

Pairing Birds

Many people are confused as to how to pair their birds. In the past, wild-caught pairs were readily available, and perfect for breeders. Now the question is, can you pair a tame, ex-pet bird with a wild-caught bird? The answer is yes! Can you pair two tame ex-pet birds together? Yes! So you see, there is much flexibility with the greys, and there are still many wild-caught singles and pairs being traded and sold these days, so there are many combinations available to bird breeders. I would caution breeders to observe any new pairs for a least several weeks WITHOUT a nest box so you can pick up on any aggressive behavior. Once the nest box is put up, it will be difficult to see how the birds are getting along, and some birds are aggressive to their mates inside the nest box. Some tame, ex-pet male Congo African Greys are obnoxious and aggressive towards the female. If this is the case with your pair, watch them carefully (always from a distance, and hopefully out of the bird's view, because you may cause them to act differently if you are in their sight). If your female cannot fight back with the male, then you may need to get a more passive male bird or a wild-caught male grey.

If you purchased the male and female separately, it is important that you introduce them properly. Start with the two birds in separate cages, and if they are in quarantine, let them see each other from opposite ends of the room. Slowly move the cages closer together, until they are side by side. Make sure that each cage has the perches mounted at the same height, so the birds can practically sit "next to each other" even though they are in separate cages. When you are ready to put the birds together, you need a third, "neutral" cage that neither bird is familiar with. The reason for this is because it reduces the chances of the birds becoming aggressive and protecting their respective cages. If the neutral cage is their breeding cage, then seal off the entrance to the nest box, so you can observe the birds for a short time before you let them have their nest box.

Cage Requirements

African Greys are unsteady flyers; most are just slightly nervous and prefer to climb around inside their cages or flights. Some greys seem to love any extra room and will glide back and forth to their perches. It has been my observation that anytime I visit a breeding facility where the birds are in flight cages 6 feet long or longer, the greys do not have high production rates in these types of cages. I am sure there are many pairs of greys breeding in cages this large, but on the average, greys prefer cages that are less than 6 feet deep. A good size breeding cage for Congos, Ghanas or Timnehs is 3-4 feet wide, 3-4 feet tall, and 3-4 feet deep. If you live in the suburbs and are cage breeding indoors, then you may need the smaller cages due to your limited space. A cage that measures 30 by 36 by 36 inches is an ideal size. A macaw-sized cage (24 by 36 inches) is also a good breeding cage for a pair of greys.

Breeders that have lots of room (either indoors or outdoors) may choose to put their birds in flight cages that measure 4 feet by 4 feet by 6 feet long. Most large breeding facilities have their breeding cages suspended at least three feet high. This way the birds do not have access to the floor, and the debris falling to the ground makes cleaning easier.

It is important to position the perches almost parallel inside the cage so that the birds will be able to fly from one perch to the other. The highest perch inside the cage should be the one that goes directly in front of the nest box.

Toys in the Breeder's Cages

African Greys love to chew, especially wood. It should not affect your productivity if you supply the birds with a simple, natural wood-type chew toy inside the breeding cage. You have to put this toy inside the cage before you put the birds inside the cage, and if they destroy the toy, it is best to put an identical toy in the same exact place. If your birds are on eggs or babies, don't mess with the cage at all; wait until you have pulled the babies for hand-rearing before you make any changes. Upsetting the birds while they are on eggs could cause them to abandon the eggs or injure the babies.

The Nest Box

The most popular style of nest box for all African Greys is the L-Shaped, or boot box. It measures 24" x 12" x 24", and there is usually a wire ladder down the inside from the opening.

Important Note: If you purchase any African Greys for breeding that still have their quarantine band on, (this type of band has an opening) then it should be removed before placing the birds into their breeding cage. This is because it is possible for the birds to get their band caught on the wire ladder inside the nest box, thus resulting in them chewing and mutilating their foot, or even death. Closed leg bands should not be a hazard, unless there are open pieces of wire in the nest box. (There shouldn't be.)

African Greys love the L-Shape, or boot nest box.

We have our nest boxes made out of 3/4 inch pine wood, because our greys love to chew their boxes. We fill the boxes with about 4 to 5 inches of pine shavings, and let the pair do the rest. Greys love to rearrange the shavings and line their nests with old feathers. Do not smooth out your grey's shavings inside of the nest-they will be disturbed by you rearranging their home.

The nest box is normally placed up high, toward the rear of the cage, so when you feed and clean your aviaries, it gives the birds a sense of security, and they will almost always dive into their boxes when you come around.

Important Note: African greys are known for being good parents and incubating their eggs. Unfortunately, they are such good parents that in very warm weather (temperatures in the nineties and higher) the eggs may get too warm and the embryos will die. If you are worried about the weather, it is best to pull the eggs for hatching and rearing; or you may switch the eggs for fake eggs and put the real eggs inside of your incubator until the heat spell passes, then you may swap eggs again and let the parents hatch them.

Feeding Your Breeders

Feeding Breeder African Grey parrots is not much different than feeding a pet African Grey. (See Chapter 5). The main difference is supplementing your pairs with extra calcium when they lay eggs and while they are feeding the babies. If you do not do this, you may experience babies with splayed legs (spraddle leg), or broken bones.

Cuttlebone: Serve your breeders fresh cuttlebone as often as they want it. If your birds will not eat the cuttlebone, then you may scrape the soft side with a knife and sprinkle the dust on your bird's fruit and vegetable bowl or seed dish.

Calcium Powder: There are several different powders being used for calcium supplementation, the most popular at this time is D-Ca-Fos®, manufactured by Fort Dodge Laboratories. D-Ca-Fos® can be sprinkled on the seeds or fruits and vegetables, and dosages vary; most breeders use approximately 1/8 teaspoon several times a week, unless a bird has a confirmed calcium deficiency.

Important Note: D-Ca-Fos® has calcium and phosphorous with vitamin D3 added, and it should be used in moderation; too much Vitamin D3 can be toxic, and your bird can become very ill or possibly die if you overdo it.

Neo-Calglucon® Syrup: Neo-Calglucon® syrup is a human calcium supplement that is available from your local pharmacy. It comes in a pint-size bottle. (Some pharmacies do not stock this item, but can order it for you.) You add the syrup to your bird's drinking water, and there is no "set" dosage, we use 1 teaspoon in a 12-ounce crock of water; most veterinarians will recommend 3cc's per 4 ounces of water.

Pellets for Breeders

There are more and more breeders converting their birds to a pelleted diet, and some of the pellets are available in a breeder formula, which is nutritionally geared for birds that are breeding. As I mentioned before, we can expect the pelleted food industry to keep growing, and as our knowledge of parrots and their nutritional needs grows, we should see a more complete pelleted diet for pets and breeders.

Some breeders don't feed their breeder birds or their offspring any seeds, I understand the purpose of their goal towards better nutrition, however, I feel it is important to teach all offspring how to crack seeds, and possibly offer seeds occasionally for recreational purposes. (Birds love to pick through seed mixtures looking for a favorite seed.)

Average Clutch Size & Frequency of Nesting

The average clutch size for African Grey parrots is two to three eggs. The female will lay an egg about every third day. The average Congo egg measures approximately $1^3/4$", the average Ghana egg $1^5/8$", and the average Timneh egg measures $1^1/2$". Four eggs is not uncommon, but not indicative of a typical clutch. African Greys will breed year 'round, and do not have a limited breeding season. The first time a pair of greys goes to nest, they will usually clutch again if the babies were pulled for hand-rearing. This is called "Double-Clutching". After the second time, the birds will usually take a rest of several months or more. If the pair nests a third time, you should seal the entrance to the nest box for at least two months to give the birds time to get back into condition. Feeding babies is hard work, and the parents get tired and their immune systems are lowered from all of their efforts. Your breeders are more susceptible to illness at this time and you need to give them a well-deserved rest.

Important Note: Don't worry if your African grey hen does not sit on her eggs right away; she may wait until she is finished laying the entire clutch. This way the eggs will hatch around the same time and the babies will usually be fed equally.

Eggs are still viable for about a week after they are laid, even if they are not incubated. Once the hen starts sitting on the egg, however, the development process starts, and then any further interruptions in incubation could affect the egg.

Some female greys will accidentally drop their first egg while sitting on the perch. This is not uncommon, and if the bird is familiar with its nest box, it should make an effort to go inside the nest box the second time around. If this happens, put a thick layer of shavings on the bottom of the cage, if possible, in case it should happen again. You may be able to salvage the egg and place it in your incubator. Anytime a bird lays an egg off the perch, it is best to artificially incubate it, because if you put it inside the nest box, chances are the pair will not acknowledge it inside the nest box if they did not put it there.

A typical pair of African Greys will produce offspring up to three times in one year. Don't get your hopes up, however; every pair of birds is different. We have one proven pair of Congo African Greys that always lay one clutch, usually only one egg once a year!

Candling the Eggs

Once the eggs are laid and the hen has started incubating, you can wait 5-7 days to check the eggs to see if they are fertile. This is commonly referred to as "candling the eggs," even though you use a small flashlight, not a candle.

The easiest way to candle the eggs is with a small, flexible flashlight. There are many types of flexible optic lights available which are also good; we simply use an auto map light, which is small and can fit in your pocket and is available at any auto supply store.

To candle the eggs, you must cover the entrance to the nest box while the pair is outside. This can be quite difficult because once the pair is on eggs they will not get off the nest often or readily. Some grey pairs will scurry out of the nest if you are there to inspect it, while others will sit tight and growl and lunge for you. If you cannot get the birds out of the nest, you will need to carefully use a magazine or book to place between the birds and the eggs. Watch your fingers! Any bird protecting its nest is likely to deliver a nasty bite. Some greys will bite their babies due to misplaced aggression (they want to bite you). So you must use caution during these situations.

To candle an egg, hold the light up to the wide end of the egg and you will see the air space and the contents.

If there are any red veins present, the egg is fertile. If the egg looks clear inside, it is probably infertile. Don't mistake streaks on the eggshell for veins. Do not throw away any egg until you are absolutely sure it is infertile; check the egg(s) 2-3 more times before pulling it, if your pair will allow it. Continue candling fertile eggs every 4-5 days to check their progress. As the embryo continues to develop, the interior of the egg becomes darker and more dense. If your light is strong, you can still see faint veins encircling the egg. Infertile eggs should be discarded by 14 days, in hopes that the pair will lay another clutch of eggs that may be fertile the next time.

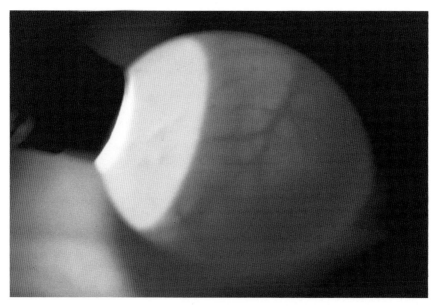

A fertile egg will show red veins around 6 or 7 days after the hen has started incubating it.

Incubating African Grey Eggs

African Greys are such prolific breeders, it is a shame to pull their eggs for incubating when they usually do such a good job. If you must incubate your African Grey eggs, or if there is an emergency and your pair abandons the nest, the ideal temperature for incubating African Grey eggs is between $98\frac{1}{2}$ to $99\frac{1}{4}$ degrees Fahrenheit. The humidity is usually fine at 46 to 50 percent, which is 81 to 83 degrees on the wet bulb. The hatching tray in the bottom of most larger incubators is slightly cooler than the shelves above, but that is normal, and should not affect hatching.

Important Note: Do NOT rely on the thermometer installed inside of your incubator to tell you what temperature it is; some of the thermometers are very poor quality, and do not give you an accurate temperature. Others are placed in locations nowhere near where the eggs will rest. The temperature could vary in different sections of the incubator, and you will not know it unless you test the temperature with a high quality mercury thermometer. A clean human thermometer will tell you how warm the temperature is, but it cannot fluctuate if the temperature drops inside. A mercury thermometer will move up or down, so you must read it from the outside of the incubator, or read it quickly when you open your incubator, because it will start to change right away.

Different incubators use different turning methods. The Turn-X® turner rolls the eggs back and forth every hour. The Humidaire® holds the eggs in a tray that rotates 45 degrees back and forth every hour. The Grumbach® slowly rolls the eggs a full 180 degrees as often as you program it to do so. Parrot eggs usually do best when they are turned 180 degrees about five times a day, alternating the direction. Never turn the eggs in the same direction; it may weaken the chick.

If you incubator rocks the eggs back and forth on a tray like the Humidaire®, you should turn each egg by hand, 180 degrees one to three times a day. To help remember which way to turn an egg, you may carefully write on the egg (with a pencil): on one side, write a letter "A" and draw an arrow pointing to the right; on the other side, write "B" and draw an arrow to the left. That way, the person who turns the egg will know which direction to move it.

Important Note: Always make sure your hands are clean when handling eggs! Bacteria and viruses can enter through the porous eggshell and harm the chicks.

The normal incubation period for African Grey eggs is 28 days. The chick will usually internally pip around 25 to 27 days, and hatching will occur within 24 to 48 hours. African Grey eggs hatch easily and usually need no assistance.

You can tell when an egg is ready to hatch, because it begins what is called internal pipping or "draw-down". The way you can check for internal pipping is to candle the egg and check the position of the air space; during normal incubation, the airspace is vertical. When the bird begins to internally pip, the air space tilts to about a 45 degree angle. The line between the air space and the chick looks less sharp, and more fuzzy.

When you are candling you may even see the shadow of the chick's beak moving up and down inside. Once the air space has tilted, the egg can be moved to the hatching tray, and you should only turn it by hand once in the morning, and once at night, if the chick is not out by then. What happens inside the egg is that the chick pips the membrane of the airspace, and breathes the air inside. Once the chick runs out of oxygen and starts breathing carbon dioxide, it starts having spasms and pushes upward to break, or pip the external eggshell. It has a tiny horn on the end of its beak called an eggtooth that helps it to break through both the membrane and the eggshell. The chick will continue to push upwards, punch the egg, and turn slightly, then continue all the way around the egg. Once the bird makes it all the way around, the top of the egg pops off and the chick very tiredly crawls out!

Within 24 hours of internal pipping you should notice an external pip or cracks in the egg shell. You should check for continuous activity with the egg for the next 24 hours. It is not uncommon for baby grey chicks to peep loudly while they are inside the egg right before hatching.

Birds That Pip Internally But Do Not Pip the Shell

This common occurance is usually caused by low humidity during incubation. If you notice the chick has not pipped externally 24 hours after internal pipping, you should make a small hole in the air space to see what's going on. Candle the egg to locate the chick. Use a plastic toothpick or a small knife (or anything that can be sterilized before using) to make a 1/4-inch size hole. Look inside. If the membrane looks white and stiff like paper, the baby is too dry and will need help hatching.

Enlarge the hole and dip a sterile cotton swab or paintbrush in warm, distilled water and lightly dab it on the membrane. Try to locate the bird's beak and see if it has torn the membrane around the beak area. If it has, try pushing back the membrane around the chick's beak and nostrils. If the baby peeps loudly, it is usually the sign of a strong chick.

Assisting a Hatch

If the chick appears slow moving, and slowly opens and closes its beak, it is probably weak from struggling against the hard membrane. Put the egg back in the incubator and moisten the membrane with warm distilled water every hour. When assisting a hatch, avoid all blood veins when peeling back the membrane. Breaking a blood vein could cause a chick to bleed to death.

Avoid the chick's nostrils, and keep trying to push back the membrane to expose the chick's beak and head. If there is any bleeding, STOP, and try again in a few hours; the chick is not ready to hatch. Continuing to assist such a hatch may kill the chick. If there is no bleeding, you may continue to peel back the shell. starting with the area over the airspace.

It is important to realize that there are no set rules to follow when it comes to hatching eggs. Each situation is different, and the guidelines in this book may not apply to your particular needs.

Once the baby's head and shoulders are exposed, turn the egg sideways so the baby can crawl out, possibly on its own. If the baby is very weak, you may need to gently lift its head out. If you do this, look inside at the chick's belly to make sure that it has absorbed all of the egg yolk. If it has not, you will see a greenish-yellow lima bean or pea-like ball stuck to the chick's belly, between its legs. If you see this, you must put the chick's head back and cap the egg with another eggshell-one that has been thoroughly cleaned and rinsed with a nontoxic disinfectant. Try to cap the egg loosely, so that air can still get in, but the baby must remain confined inside the egg. If you don't have or want to use an eggshell, you can use plastic wrap that has been disinfected and poked with several holes. Be sure to poke the holes before placing it loosely over the end of the egg. Leave the egg alone for 6-8 hours and then check it again (moisten if necessary). If the yolk is still visible, then you must wait. If the yolk has been absorbed when you check again, you may leave the egg uncapped and continue assisting in the hatch.

The baby may still be connected to the egg by a thin cord to its umbilicus. Allow the chick to naturally break this. There will also be a small mass of green to clear waste products inside the egg. The first time a baby passes a stool, it is bright green and thick looking. This should not be confused with the waste products in the shell. But you may see both in the shell after a baby hatches.

Chapter 17

Care and Feeding of Grey Babies

Babies in the Nest

If you decide to leave the babies with the parents, it is your responsibility to see that they do a good job. You must check on the babies every day, preferably an hour after you put out fresh food and water, because if the parents are regularly feeding the babies, the babies will be fed at this time.

The babies' crops should be partially or completely full when you check. The babies should be in an upright position and their skin should be light pink. If the babies are hungry, they will cry to be fed. If they are full, they will be sleepy and quiet. If you are not sure the parents are caring for the babies, feel them, and if they are cool to the touch, pull them immediately for hand-rearing. If the baby appears weak, and you suspect it has not been fed, pull it.

Assuming the parents have fed the babies, the best time to pull baby greys for hand-rearing is when their eyes start slitting open, which is around 11 days. If you have a clutch of three babies, pull them when the middle baby's eyes are opening. It will not make a difference if a baby's eyes have been open several days, or even a week, before it is pulled.

Brooders for Day-1 Grey Babies

Hopefully you will not need to pull your babies at Day-1, but in the event you do, you should have a brooder ready. The temperature inside the brooder (remember to double check with another thermometer!) should be around 98 degrees Fahrenheit. After the chick is about seven to ten days old, gradually lower the temperature, approximately two to four degrees each week. If there is more than one baby in the clutch, the babies generate heat and huddle together. If the babies are too cold, they will feel cool to the touch, and will shiver; if the babies are too warm, they will separate and spread out. Continue gradually adjusting the temperature in your brooder unit until you find one that suits the group of babies.

Important Note: African grey babies are extra-sensitive to too much heat, and if they are too hot, you will see pale pink blood stain in their urine. Occasionally this will also occur if there is too much protein in their hand-feeding formula, but it is usually due to too much heat. Immediately lower your temperature and the bleeding will stop. There are no known long-term affects if this happens.

Brooders for Parent-fed Grey Babies

Babies fed by their parents usually weigh more, cry less often, and maintain their body temperatures better than babies that are hand-reared from Day-1. If your babies cry all the time, they may be too warm. Some babies cry when they are hungry and even after they are fed. This crying is different from when they are too warm, which is a more distressful call, and usually the babies will move around at the same time.

These parent-fed Congo African greys are not the cutest things unless you are lucky enough to find them inside your nest box!

Parent-fed babies do not need as much heat, so you can put them inside a homemade brooder made out of a dishtub, or small rectangular storage bucket. Line the tub with newspaper, then use a non-toxic substrate material, such as shredded newspaper or Carefresh®. Be sure you use enough substrate material, so the babies feet do not slip on the newspaper. You can even smooth out a little "nest" in the bedding and put the babies in the middle.

You may also take a small towel, roll it up, and place it around the nest. Be sure to use towels that are smooth, and have no loose terry loops that the birds can get their nails caught on.

For warmth, you may place a heating pad down the side of the tub. Always use the "Low" setting on the heating pad; anything else is too hot. To make the tub even cozier, you can drape a towel over half of the tub, so the babies can huddle underneath. When the babies get older (around 4-6 weeks) they will pull the towel down, or prefer the open side. At this time I will only cover the tub at night.

Important Note: African grey babies are famous for their "chicken scratch" they will put their head down (many times in a corner) and scratch with their feet, like they are trying to dig a hole in their bedding, or cage. Most babies start this around 4-5 weeks of age, and usually outgrow it when they wean off their hand-feeding formula. Some adult birds will do it occasionally; sometimes if they are sexually mature they will start to do it in a corner of their cage. It is not exactly known why baby African Greys do this, however, it may be some instinctive behavior from nature: maybe if they are inside the nest it is a way to push away fecal matter.

If you have a cage with a grill, you will avoid a giant mess on your floor!

Hand-feeding the Babies

Day-1 babies are still absorbing their egg yolk and should not be fed solid foods for about 24 hours, or until they stop passing dark green feces. You may feed these babies a few drops of warm water, Pedialyte® or Lactated Ringers Solution every 2-3 hours. Babies will begin passing urine only when they have absorbed their egg yolk, as long as they are being fed fluids.

Important Note: It is very easy to aspirate (choke) a bird when you are feeding it straight liquids. Use an eyedropper or a small syringe and dribble small amounts of the liquid in order to prevent this from happening.

Babies that are parent-fed and pulled from the nest may be fed as soon as their crops are empty, or near empty. When the parents feed the babies, their crops are enormous, and they are full of lumpy seeds, nuts or pellets. If you feel the crop itself (and you should) it feels like there is gravel inside! This is completely normal, and the feces of the bird may look a little chunky, also.

It is okay to feed the birds even if the crop is not completely empty (but it is slowly going down) because you don't want the babies to become dehydrated.

You may use a syringe or a spoon to hand-feed your babies. A 35cc syringe with a catheter tip is best to start with; later, when the babies are eating more, you may wish to use a 60cc catheter tip syringe. Whatever you use, be sure you soak it in a safe disinfectant and rinse it thoroughly before using it. Spoon-feeding takes longer and is messier, but if you are uncomfortable with a syringe, start out with the spoon.

You will need to decide if you are going to use your own recipe for hand-feeding, or if you are going to purchase a ready-to-use instant formula. African greys grow well and seem to thrive on almost all of the major brands of hand-feeding formula, so it really is not necessary to make your own. It is important to check your hand-feeding formula for freshness, and I like to freeze my dry formula until I'm ready to use it. I do not recommend keeping any bird food in the freezer longer than 6 months.

Hand-feeding Technique / Syringe Feeding

Hand-feeding is another way of saying syringe-feeding. It is actually better understood if it is referred to as syringe-feeding. So many aviculturists have adopted the phrase, "hand-feeding" that it is confusing to beginners, who picture a baby bird licking formula from the breeder's hand. Tube feeding is also different, because it involves attaching a soft rubber tube to the tip of the syringe, to insert into the bird's esophagus (or food pipe). Grey babies are so easy to feed I will not discuss tube feeding, because the only time you would need to tube feed a grey is if it was ill, and your veterinarian would need to show you how to do it.

Proper Syringe-Feeding Technique

If you are right handed, hold the baby's head with your left hand, with your thumb on one side of the beak and forefinger on the other side of the beak. If you are left handed, hold the baby's head with your right hand and feed with your left.

Insert the syringe into the baby's mouth. Each time you feed, try to alternate feeding from the right or left side. Baby greys do not usually have a problem with crooked beaks from feeding on one side, however, it's a good habit to get into.

Birds instinctively show a strong feeding response (bobbing) because in the nest the parents regurgitate food from their crop into the baby's crop.

The baby instinctively closes its windpipe, lessening the possibility of aspiration. If you are syringe-feeding your baby, you are only going to insert the syringe into the mouth, right above the tongue, and you may feed from either side.

Baby greys are the best birds to learn how to hand-feed because they take little "bites" and they bob their heads up and down very gently so you get used to the motions. Some very young babies will jerk convulsively during or right after a feeding-don't worry, this is an involuntary action, and they seem to outgrow this by about 4 weeks of age.

When you insert the syringe into the baby grey's mouth, be sure to start the flow of formula, so the bird does not become confused or associate breathing when it should be eating. Take the syringe out of the bird's mouth completely so it may breathe, and learn to eat correctly.

If you are apprehensive when you feed your baby grey with a syringe, feed it small amounts with a lot of breaks, or use a spoon. It is less likely you will aspirate (choke) a baby if you feed it small amounts of food at a time, or if you use a spoon.

Amount to Feed

It is very difficult to be specific when it comes to determining what amount of formula is the correct amount. African greys are very famous for regurgitating their formula if they are too full, however, this may also be a sign of sour crop or a bacterial infection, so be sure it is not a health problem first.

Think of the bird's crop as a measuring tool. The skin of the crop is very pliable and easily stretched, so you don't want to overfeed, because then the crop becomes pendulous or stretched out. On the other hand, some people starve their birds because they don't realize the baby's crop is empty. The folds of skin in the crop sometimes look like there is a small amount of food present. Fortunately, baby greys usually have very tight crops, and there is no doubt when your babies are empty.

In the wild, and in the nest, parent birds never wait until the baby's crop is empty before feeding; they feed the baby, whether the crop is empty or not. If your baby has a small amount of food in its crop the next time you want to feed it, go ahead and feed it at that time. You may wish to feed slightly less formula so it will be ready for its next scheduled feeding. When a bird digests its food too slowly, it may have sour crop, or a bacterial infection.

Feeding Guidelines:

Baby Congos & Ghanas fed from Day-1:

Day 1-3   Feed every $1^1/_2$ to 2 hours, approx. $^1/_2$-2 cc's.
Day 4-13   Feed every $2^1/_2$ to 3 hours, approx. 3 - 10 cc's.
Day 14-21   Feed every 4 hours, approx. 10-18 cc's.
Day 22-35   Feed every 5 hours, approx. 18-40 cc's.
Day 36 -   Feed every 8-12 hours, up to 60 cc's, and
Weaning   decreasing at weaning.

Baby Congos & Ghanas Parent Fed
for the first two weeks:

Day 14-21   Feed every 4 hours, approx. 10-20 cc's.
Day 22-35   Feed every 6 hours, approx. 25-50 cc's.
Day 36-   Feed every 8-12 hours, up to 60 cc's and
Weaning   decreasing at weaning.

Baby Timnehs fed from Day-1:

Day 1-3   Feed every 1-2 hours, approx. $^1/_2$ - $1^1/_2$ cc's.
Day 4-13   Feed every 2-3 hours, approx. 2-8 cc's.
Day 14-21   Feed every 3-4 hours, approx. 7-15 cc's.
Day 22-35   Feed every 5 hours, approx. 15-30 cc's.
Day 36-   Feed every 8 hours, approx. 30-40 cc's, and
Weaning   decreasing at weaning.

Baby Timnehs Parent Fed
for the first two weeks:

Day 14-21   Feed every 4 hours, approx. 10-20 cc's.
Day 22-35   Feed every 6 hours, approx. 20-30 cc's.
Day 36-   Feed every 8 hours, approx. 35 cc's and
Weaning   decreasing at weaning.

Important Note: These guidelines are approximations for an average African Grey baby; your baby's needs may vary accordingly.

Choosing a Formula

African Grey babies seem to thrive on most of the major brands of ready to use hand-feeding formulas. Use a formula with 8 percent fat, because the 12 percent fat formulas are designed for South American birds, and it is not necessary with the African birds.

Check with your avian veterinarian, or an experienced breeder for a recommendation when it comes to a hand-feeding formula. Keep in mind that hand-feeding formulas are very trendy, and many aviculturists periodically switch from one brand to another for their own personal reasons.

Once you open a can or bag of hand-feeding formula, you may keep it in the refrigerator. If you would like to keep extra bags of formula in your freezer, I feel comfortable freezing the powdered formula for six months or less.

Adding Additional Ingredients to Instant Formulas

It is not necessary to add a lot of extra ingredients to an already complete commercially prepared food. If you like to add a lot of different items, you may as well prepare your own recipe, because if you dilute the ready-to-use hand-feeding formulas too much, you lose the effects of the vitamins and other nutrients in the formula. A general rule of thumb is to add no more than 20 percent of the total volume of food.

Adding extra vitamins is dangerous, too, because you can easily over vitaminize your babies. This results in stunting, poor feather quality, stress lines on the bird's feathers, and possibily more serious health problems.

Adding Antibiotics to Formula

Never add antibiotics to your baby greys' formula as a preventative measure. This only lowers the bird's resistance to additional bacteria, and it allows the bacteria to build a resistance to that particular drug so the drug may not be effective later.

We add antibiotics to the formula only when a baby is ill, and we have cultured the chick to find out which drug is sensitive to the bacteria that is the culprit. Each antibiotic is different, but sometimes it is more effective to administer a small amount of baby food with the antibiotic one hour before a full feeding is scheduled. This way the bird's crop has a chance to quickly absorb the medicine.

Weighing Babies

When you hand-feed one or more grey babies, weigh each one daily to check its progress. Be sure you weigh a chick when its crop is empty, and at the same time each day, so you can get an accurate pattern for growth. Until weaning, your babies should gain weight every day. If you feel the keel bone (the bone that runs down the center of the bird below the crop), you can get a general idea if a bird is thin.

The bird's chest muscles should be firm on each side of the keel bone, and the bone should only protrude slightly. Weighing a baby, however, is the best way to catch a potential health problem.

You don't have to buy the most expensive scale, but try to get the most accurate one available for your budget. We use a triple-beam balance scale, which is accurate to 1/10 of a gram. (One pound equals 454 grams.)

If you need to take your grey to the veterinarian, be sure to take your weight charts with you. Birds that gain weight slowly or not at all, especially when they are very young, are almost always ill, and if they are not seen and treated by a veterinarian as soon as you notice a problem, they will usually die.

Important note: Baby greys that are fully feathered and weaning off their hand-feeding formula may lose approximately 10-15% of their total body weight. This is normal, and as long as the bird looks and acts healthy and is not underweight, it is not a problem.

Introducing Babies to Soft Foods

Baby greys may be given soft foods and millet spray when they are feathered on 50 percent or more of their bodies. Start weaning them from the hand-feeding formula when they are fully feathered. When you serve fresh fruits and vegetables, cut them in LARGE pieces, so the bird cannot swallow them whole. They will scrape bite size pieces off the big pieces! Do not feed frozen mixed vegetables or canned vegetables because they spoil very quickly. Here's a list of foods to serve to weaning baby greys:

- Rice cakes
- Unsalted crackers
- Wheat bread (plain or toasted)
- Cheerios®
- Large pieces of fruits and vegetables
- Millet spray
- Pelleted food

When the baby is feathered over 90 percent of its body, you may also put a dish of seed and a small dish of water in its cage. The chick will play with the seeds and get them dirty, but that's okay. Just be sure to change the seed frequently. You want the baby to get used to having seed around. It will soon start sampling different seeds. The first time the baby drinks, it may cough or sneeze; this is normal.

Baby birds try to "guzzle" the water as if it were hand-feeding formula, and they need to learn how to lap it slowly. If this happens, take the water away, and reintroduce the bird to water in a few days.

By the time a baby grey is fully feathered, it will start refusing to hand-feed, or it will regurgitate (spit up) some of its formula immediately after you feed it. Greys are normally very easy to wean, because they do not usually get too attached to their hand-feeding syringe. Many wean themselves by eating less and less formula and walking away from the syringe when they are full. If this happens, do not try to follow the bird around so you can get it to eat its full feeding. A small percentage of greys really do like hand-feeding, and they would do it forever if their owners let them! If this is the case, be sure the bird is eating a large variety of foods and is drinking water, and then slowly start weaning it off the morning feeding, then do the same with the evening feeding.

Birds That Refuse to Wean

Some birds will hand-feed as long as possible because they enjoy the ritual, and others will do so because they are ill. A chick that refuses to wean should be taken to your veterinarian for a check-up and a culture and sensitivity. If the bird is sick, or has a sub-clinical bacteria, it is best to treat the bird with antibiotics before weaning it. If it is not sick, then you may gradually start to wean the bird off its hand-feeding formula.

If a healthy bird is hand-feeding three times a day, gradually cut down to two feedings, twelve hours apart. For example, if your 12 week-old grey baby is eating 35-40 cc's three times a day, start reducing the middle feeding and slightly increase the morning and evening feeding. So now the bird may eat 45 cc's in the morning, and 45-50 cc's in the evening. If the bird is eating some seeds, fruits and vegetables, and pellets, then that is a good sign. You may then start to reduce the morning feeding 5 cc's each day, until you are no longer feeding the bird in the morning. DO NOT increase the evening feeding when you do this! Fortunately, African greys have very tight crops, and it is very difficult to overfeed them.

Once the bird is only hand-feeding at night, then you may start to reduce the amount fed each night by 5 cc's. The bird may have already not wanted to eat the full amount of formula at night; if this is the case, you are almost there! Otherwise, continue feeding less and less formula each night. The last time you plan to hand-feed the bird you may wish to wash the hand-feeding syringe and give it to the bird to chew up.

When you do this, it is important to tell the bird that he or she is "all grown up now" and no longer needs to eat like a baby. Once they chew up the syringe, you will be less likely to want to hand-feed the bird, which is a common reason birds will not wean, because their owners are not quite ready!

Important note: Some bird owners like to keep an extra hand-feeding syringe in their home for two reasons: (1) Some veterinarians and bird lovers like to periodically feed their adult birds from the syringe as a treat; (2) If your bird should need oral medication, the syringe may come in handy. If you should need a syringe and your veterinarian or bird store is closed, you can purchase a children's medicine syringe in your local drugstore—they work just fine.

During and after weaning, it is important that you weigh your baby grey. A slight weight loss is to be expected, but if the baby just doesn't seem to be doing well, then by all means resume additional feedings and consult your veterinarian. If you plan on breeding African Greys and feeding lots of babies, after feeding several clutches, you will be able to tell if the bird's weights are good just by feeling the birds and looking at them.

Once your baby is weaned, you can weigh it once a week if you like, or just feel its keel bone.

Problems Common With Baby African Greys

There are a few recurring health problems that seem to be more common with African Grey babies. These are: shaking/shuddering, blood in the urine, leg deformities, and twisted neck.

Baby Shakes or Shudders

Young babies (a few days to approximately 3 weeks old) may shake or shudder, especially after a feeding. If this is the first time you have fed African Grey babies, you may notice that they are almost convulsive in their movements. This is usually not a health-related problem, but a behavior which usually disappears as the babies get older and more coordinated.

Blood in the Urine

The first time I had a clutch of baby greys and this happened I really got scared; the entire newspaper underneath their shavings (we didn't have Carefresh at that time) was pink!

I immediately called my veterinarian, who fortunately also raised many birds, including African Greys, and he told me that they were either too warm, or had too much protein in their hand-feeding formula. At the time we were using a recipe that we mixed in the blender, and we did use High Protein Baby Cereal. I also had them in a brooder with a heating pad on the bottom, and they looked kind of hot. So I substituted the Rice Cereal for High Protein Baby Cereal, and I re-positioned my heating pad down the side of the brooder (which was a dish pan). Within hours my birds were perfect!

If you have a similar situation, it must be corrected right away, or your birds may develop more serious health problems. If they are only overheated for a short time, then there is usually no harm to the birds.

Leg Deformities

Some African Grey babies have spraddle leg, or broken bones at a very early age. This usually happens in the nest, while the parents are feeding and caring for the babies. Many leg problems are actually fractures sustained while the birds are very young, which is called a "Green stick fracture." They are called this because the bones are soft and bendable, like a young branch on a tree. Sometimes bones are broken, and unless you look closely, you cannot tell.

Spraddle leg, and multiple fractures are usually indicative of a vitamin and/or calcium deficiency. Sometimes the parents only feed their babies the least nutritious foods, such as seeds and nuts. That is why it is so important to sprinkle vitamins and calcium on the parents' seeds and fruits and vegetables. Don't overdo it, but be sure that they will somehow get some of the vitamins. If your birds refuse to eat food that has powdered vitamins on it, then you can use a water soluable vitamin for their drinking water. Also serve the pair as much cuttlebone as they will eat when they are laying eggs and feeding babies.

It is crucial that you correct leg deformities as early as possible, while the bones are still soft. Occasionally you may need to wait until a baby grey is older and it may need surgery to correct an old break. I recently experienced this with a baby that I let the parents feed for 10 days. I did not follow through in making sure to give them plenty of vitamins or calcium, and they are "seed junkies" anyway. There were two babies in the clutch, but the male bit one when I took it out of the nest (I had a magazine blocking the parents, but the male stuck his head around it unexpectedly and misplaced his aggressions towards me onto his offspring).

In addition to a severe bite on the neck, this baby had obvious leg problems. Then I looked at the other clutchmate and it had leg problems also. The first baby died, unfortunately, but the second baby worried me. I sprinkled D-Ca-Fos® into his hand-feeding formula twice a day, and waited for it to grow a little more, so I could figure out what was wrong. It turned out that both legs had green stick fractures; one was much worse than the other. I am sure that it was mostly nutritional, and partially overzealous parents.

Because the damage was too severe to correct with a splint, I had to wait until the baby was five weeks old so my avian veterinarian could perform surgery on the bad leg. The "good" leg was improving, so I was glad my poor baby didn't need surgery for both! It is important to understand something about when birds break a bone: (1) The bone will start to heal immediately, and within 3-5 days it will heal in the position it is in, whether it is correct or incorrect, and (2) If you re-break a bone, when it heals, it deposits extra calcium at the site of the break, and that can offset a prior fracture.

I have never had a baby bird of any type need surgery at such a young age, and I was nervous for my bird. The veterinarian that performed the surgery, however, had just performed a similar surgery on a cockatoo, and he was confident that it should go well. I was able to take the bird home the same day, and he was perky and almost cute in a full leg "cast" (really gauze and vet wrap from ankle to hip).

One week after the surgery, we unwrapped the "cast" to check out the leg. There was a lot of swelling in the baby's toes, so we wanted to be sure the bandage wasn't too tight. (Bandaging baby birds is difficult because they grow so quickly.) When we took the bandage off, the leg looked like rubber. My veterinarian made another "cast", only this time with pieces of a tongue depressor on each side of the leg to act as a solid splint. One week later I removed this splint, and the leg looked pretty good. Our next obstacle was now the two rear toes on the foot of the injured leg; they kept folding forward, and the bird was not spreading its toes on that foot. I made a sling with vet-wrap and taped the toes backwards. I kept taping the two toes until the bird was 12 weeks old. Between 12 and 14 weeks of age, the bird began to grip the perch correctly, and climb and hang upside down in his cage. The procedure was a success!

The author's baby grey at four weeks of age. Note the serious fracture on the right leg.

Photo by Gail Worth

The author's baby grey at twelve weeks of age. The bird has a slight difference in grip with its right foot, and it will always step with a slight hesitation, but otherwise the bird is normal.

Important Note: Birds that are handicapped or birds that have recuperated from situations similar to my bird make excellent pets. Of course, their price should be considerably less, and their health history should be fully disclosed to the new owner. (Imagine purchasing a bird that didn't look quite right and not knowing the bird was treated for an injury or similar situation.)

Baby's Neck is Twisted All or Most of the Time

A grey baby may sleep with its head tucked behind it, but if your baby seems to have its head tilted or neck twisted, you must have it examined by your veterinarian. The bird should be checked for a bacterial or respiratory infection and sometimes a "neck brace" may be recommended in addition to antibiotics.

It is very important that you try to arrange the baby's bed so the chick does not favor laying its head on one side. If you catch it early, all you need to do is prop the baby's head so it cannot tilt. You can help brace a young chick's neck with soft rolls of tissue.

Excessive head tilt problems can be permanent, so try all options while the bird is young and flexible. If you continue to raise babies with problems, you may need to review your techniques in incubation, hand-rearing and diet.

Conclusion

It is my hope that all owners of African Greys are able to better understand their birds emotional, as well as physical needs. Because these birds are so intelligent, they are more "emotionally needy" than some birds. Meeting these needs, and not overindulging our precious pets, should be our goal.

There are many people successfully breeding African Grey parrots, and I do not see any threat to their captive breeding population in the near nor in the distant future.

I have purposely tried not to make statements regarding the care and upbringing of African Greys that imply one specific diet, training method, or cage size must be utilized. When it comes to birds, many different methods are acceptable, and it is very confusing when you read something that contradicts the last book or article you read.

Finally, I hope I have communicated how important it is to acknowledge your pet African Grey by really trying to "talk" to it. You may feel funny at first talking to your bird, or you may already do it all the time, but the point is that you will be able to send messages and enhance the level of communication with your grey, or any bird that you use these same techniques on. Birds really are one of the most amazing pets you can own, and I feel that the more we try to learn about them, the better.

I would like to thank all of my friends and clients that responded to my survey, and especially thank all of you who encouraged me and patiently waited for me to finish this book!

Manufacturer Information

Avia® Vitamins
Nutra-Vet Research Corporation   Phone: (914) 473-1900
201 Smith Street
Poughkeepsie, NY 12601

Super Preen® Vitamins
Blair's Super Preen Products   Phone: (800) 421-8239
1640 East Edinger Avenue, Unit 1
Santa Ana, CA 92705

Nekton® Vitamins
Nekton U.S.A.   Phone: (813) 530-3500
14405 60th Street North
Clearwater, FL 34620

D-Ca-Fos®
Fort Dodge Laboratories   Phone: (913) 664-7000
9401 Indian Creek Parkway
Building 40, Suite 1500
Overland Park, KS 66210

Pro-feda®
Vitakraft Pet Products Co., Inc.   Phone: (908) 560-7400
Chimney Rock Road, Building 12 E
Bound Brook, NJ 08805

Neon® Cages & Playpens
Cockatoo & Parrot Shampoo®
Enviro-Clean® Disinfectant
Neon Pet Products, Inc.   Phone: (714) 670-7302
15919 Phoebe Avenue   FAX: (714) 562-1747
La Mirada, California 90630

Carefresh® Pet Bedding
Absorption Corp.   Phone: (800) 242-2287
P.O. Box 5667   FAX: (360) 671-1588
Bellingham, WA 98227

Additional Sources of Information*

A newsletter just for African Grey Lovers:

The Grey Play Round Table
FDR Station, P.O. Box 1744
New York, NY 10150-1744

$18 per year (4 issues) U.S., For Canada $20 U.S., Foreign $25 U.S.

A video just for African Grey Lovers:

The Total Grey
Post Office Box 8401
Long Beach, CA 90808

$34 check or money order (shipping & handling included)

A non-profit national organization that is dedicated solely to avicultural pursuits with a mandate to protect and defend one's rights to keep birds:

American Federation of Aviculture
Post Office Box 56218
Phoenix, AZ 85079-6218
(602) 484-0931

Various membership rates; individual membership: $30 (Foreign members add $16) Includes subscription to the AFA Watchbird Magazine.

* Prices are as of 10/95 should be confirmed before sending in orders.

A non-profit international organization that strives to protect, preserve and enhance the keeping and breeding of exotic birds and the funding of avian research:

International Aviculturists Society
P.O. Box 280383
Memphis, TN 38168

Phone: (901) 872-7612

Various memberships; Individual member: $25 annually, includes a subscription to Cage Bird Hobbyist Magazine.

Veterinarian Information Sources

Association of Avian Veterinarians
AAV Central Office
Post Office Box 811720
Boca Raton, FL 33481

Phone: (407) 393-8901
FAX: (407) 393-8902

The Association of Avian Veterinarians can refer you to a veterinarian in your area that is a member.

International Veterinary Acupuncture Society
Meredith L. Snader, V.M.D.-Public Relations Director
2140 Conestoga Road
Chester Springs, PA 19425

Phone: (610) 827-7245

Call or write for a referral for a veterinarian certified in acupuncture in your area.

American Holistic Veterinary Medical Association
2214 Old Emmorton Road
Bel Air, MD 21015

Send a self-addressed, stamped envelope for a referral for a veterinarian in your area that practices holistic medicine.